WINDOWS
Healing and Helping Through Loss

by Mary Joe Hannaford
and Michael Popkin

Published by Active Parenting, Inc., Atlanta, Georgia
ISBN 0-9618020-9-X

To those whom I have lost:

To my sister—who often supplemented my mother's role by nurturing me, loving us all in a childlikeness that kept life beautiful in its simplicity.

To my mom—who gave us all a model for living creatively and graciously, always loving the beautiful.

To my dad—who showed us that loving was a willingness to make sacrifices and spent his latter years focused on that kind of giving for my education.

To those present:

To my husband—who always encourages the expression of my deep creative needs.

To my children—who have given me the privilege and pride of parenthood as they are developing into truly creative people.

To my beautiful grandson—for whom I wish growth and development of the inner self as he captures the beauty within.

To all those hundreds of people who have shared my losses and who have honored me by sharing their losses with me.

Mary Joe Hannaford

Acknowledgments

This material is an expression of many years of influence by those who have shared their personal losses with me or have encouraged me professionally and in my own personal development.

I especially recognize the hundreds of children, teachers, school counselors and friends who have taught me so much about the importance of grieving. My memory will always reflect the beginning of this material from my first workshop on grieving for Alaska school counselors and social workers, and the impact it brought on my travels across the country. Appreciation is also due to those who have through the last eight years invited me to lead workshops for a variety of groups.

Especially, I want to recognize Sherry Stahler, an outstanding elementary school counselor, who worked closely with me and highly influenced the development of Part II; along with Beth Weiss, a mother and Girl Scout staff member who served as my first editor. I am also grateful to Paula Davis, Barbara Douglas, Betty Young, and Jackie Perry, who all read the manuscript in its early stages and encouraged me to continue.

Others who have influenced me are Dr. Gus Verdery, leader in pastoral theology (deceased), who walked the road of grief with me; Dr. Ed Nash, pastoral counselor, who has listened; Dr. Charlie Shedd, minister and author, who kept encouraging me to write; and Dr. Paul Spiegl, surgeon, who unknowingly inspired the first draft.

Most of all, of course, I am grateful to Dr. Michael Popkin, friend and publisher, who listened sensitively to my first proposal and who, in his brilliant, creative purpose, has expanded the ideas to the present form. I am also indebted to his Director of Product Development, Sue Greathead, who has been a caring, faithful editor, inspirer, encourager, idea person and contact through it all. The Active Parenting staff has been an enthusiastic partner in this production: Amy, Lou-Ann, Jim, Lisa, Nancy, Cynthia, Susan and Susan. In addition, my appreciation to Norm, who designed the cover, and my daughter Joey, who did the calligraphy, along with many more who have worked behind the scenes and shared my belief in the importance of this material.

Mary Joe Hannaford

Photographs by Julie Fletcher

Table of Contents

Windows
Misty, foggy windows
Enmeshed in raindrops
Clouded dreams
Filled with despair
Blinded
By darkened windows.

Windows
Clear, revealing windows
Enveloped with sun
Hope arising
Light emerging, changing visions
Seeing, healing
Through opened windows.

Mary Joe Hannaford

Through the window, I watched the sunset reflecting on riverboats as the lights of the city across the water began to illuminate the darkness. A whole new picture emerged as I mused on the manner in which windows have influenced our lives. There have been bay windows, dormer windows, sliding windows and stained glass windows—all with one focus—to give a view. "I would like a window with a view" is often heard in restaurants or at the registration desk of hotels. "I would like to see something beautiful."

That is how it is with life—wanting to see something beautiful. But oftentimes the view is clouded or fogged, rainy or hazy. Sometimes the view is sunny, overlooking lakes or mountains, gardens and trees; and even though we can't touch, we can see; we can connect with nature through the window. Perhaps this is part of the mixed message of windows that keeps us in touch with a world we cannot fully reach or control. They provide visual openings to our deserts as well as our gardens. They keep us in touch with our disappointments and dreams.

The Windows program provides the same mixed blessing: a time to look at loss, to touch the dark places, and a time to look at life—the blessings of sunlight that draw us like a magnet past the darkness of sorrow and into the light of recovery.

Introduction

Loss is an experience which touches us all. And death is not the only cause of our losses. We lose friends who move away; we lose the innocence associated with childhood as we grow older and wiser; we lose our sense of security in economically hard times. The list could go on. Life is so full of change that most of us face loss regularly, although we sometimes never stop to consider what is happening to us.

We have written this book for two reasons: To help you heal following a personal loss, and to enable you to help others who have experienced a loss.

In **Part I**, we will focus on your own needs as one who has lost. You will learn to identify losses in your life and have an opportunity to think about your reactions to those losses— your patterns of coping and the stages of grieving you went through. Learning to recognize meaning in life's experiences brings richness by helping you understand the temporary nature of life and the manner in which you react. Knowing your patterns can also help you throughout life as you face additional losses. The ultimate goal of this material is to assist you in finding meaning in loss and, in spite of the pain, making the experience a learning one. As you work through the material alone or with a group, follow the format in a progressive manner relating the activities to specific incidents.

Part II is designed to assist you in helping others who are experiencing loss. As you find comfort for yourself, you will also find comfort in empathizing with others, sharing those deep parts of yourself which connect you with them. This section will assist you when you just don't know what to say. It will help you to develop listening skills, teach you effective ways to offer comfort and to raise your awareness of the needs of others so that you will have more confidence as a helping person. You will be better qualified to help others identify their losses, accept the stages of grief which they are experiencing as normal and discover the learning opportunity in the loss.

May this material be a comfort as we travel this journey of life together.

Part I

When You Have Lost

I have loved
It was beauty.
I have lost
It was hell.
I have survived
It was growth.
I have recovered
It is heaven.

◆

Mary Joe Hannaford

Chapter 1

What Have You Lost?

Everything we have and everybody we love are simply on loan for a little while. Thus, each moment is precious because it is fleeting.

◆ Joyce Rupp,
Praying Our Goodbyes [1]

The Amethyst Ring

When I left for college, my father gave me a family heirloom—a beautiful amethyst ring set in heavy gold, a pink kind of gold that we rarely see anymore. I wore the ring with great pride. Now you must understand that I went to a "proper, denominational" girls' school which had a very strict honor code. One day as I left my dormitory room to cross campus to the swimming pool, I left the ring and $40—a lot of money in my day—on top of my dresser.

The $40 had been saved sacrificially by my parents to fund a summer trip for me to a church camp in the North Carolina mountains. Four of my friends were going, and we had planned a gala week together. When I returned from the pool, neither my ring nor the $40 was on the dresser. I panicked. My mind stormed, "They can't be gone! I know I left them right here. Could I have put them in a drawer? Maybe my roommate put them away?" The search went on—through drawers, under items on the

dresser, through purses. Nowhere were there any signs of the ring or the money.

My roommate returned shortly from class. In shock, I told her about the disappearance of the two items. Together we searched the room, going over every possibility. Finally, we looked at each other. I burst into tears. My

family heirloom was gone. There had been other thefts in our dorm—I just didn't think it would happen to me.

How angry I was at the thief. How angry I was at myself! I should have known better than to leave the ring out. What would I tell my dad? How could I tell my parents that I had been so careless with the money? A strange emptiness came over me as if I were trapped inside a dark cloud. My roommate and I realized that we must report the incident to the dean of women. With her arm around me, my roommate comforted me as we walked across campus. The dean heard the story through my tears. There was little comfort offered. We returned to the room. Disbelief kept returning as I reviewed the event, searching my brain to discover some solution other than admitting that the ring and money were gone. I went downstairs to the dormitory phone to tell my parents.

Over the years, I have never quite forgotten the loss of the family heirloom. My parents once again sent the $40, even more sacrificially this time. I went appreciatively with my friends to the summer camp. A number of years later, I replaced the ring. I found one in an antique shop in Charleston, South Carolina, which gave me great pleasure—but somehow, it was not quite the same. It was not a family treasure, and it did not represent my dad.

Recognizing Losses

All of us are in some way dealing with loss in our lives. Loss occurs whenever we experience a change which requires giving up familiar patterns.

We can all identify obvious changes such as death, divorce, separation, or the loss of a favorite possession like the amethyst ring. But we may have difficulty discovering losses such as moving, or losing dreams or ideals. These less obvious losses can also be significant in our lives. It has been said that every love story ends in tragedy—certainly in eventual separation. For surely if we love long enough, we shall lose everybody and everything. Either we will leave or they will leave. But somehow in it all we survive and can gain from the joy of loving, understanding more deeply that it is truly "better to have loved and lost than never to have loved at all."

Grief is a part of all human experience and a natural expression of deep sadness. We face minor grief almost daily as we experience the routine losses of life. Healing comes when we learn to identify these losses, understand our reaction patterns, accept the normal stages of grieving and come to a point of acceptance by finding new meaning which leads to recovery. Traveling through the mainstream of loss eventually brings a form of comfort, clarity and wholeness.

Think back about the story of the amethyst ring.

What was the major loss? _____

_____

What was the first reaction? _____

_____

What other reactions did you notice? _____

_____

Who comforted her? _____

_____

Besides the ring and the money, what else was lost? _____

_____

_____

_____

What do you think was gained from the experience? _____

_____

_____

_____

_____

Some Losses and Causes of Loss

The truth is that life is difficult, rarely reasonable, sometimes unfair, complex, rich.

Death of a loved one	Heritage	Identity
Money	Roots	Activity
Separation	Reputation	Agility
Power	Culture	Responsibility
Divorce	Leadership	Terminal illness
Position	Job/Career	Goals
Pets	Followers	Faculties
Title	Retiring	Dreams
Things	Success	Vision
Just leaving	Changing	Time
Fire	Failure	Speech
Loss of friends	Promotion	Structure
Theft	Change	Taste
Misplacement	Demotion	Freedom
Argument	Challenge	Sexuality
Graduating	Closing out	Independence
Distance	Stimulation	Bodily controls
Tasks	Virginity	Country
Skills	Co-workers	Surgery
Family changes	Fertility	Abortion
Elections	Location (moving)	Body parts
Growing up	Beauty	Miscarriage
Projects	Self-esteem	Teeth
Marriages	Schools	Toys
Teachers	Youth	Hair
Births	Lifestyle	Choices
Beliefs	Childhood	Appearance
Values	Faith	Energy
Leaders	Health	Stamina
Aging	Control	Trust

Primary Losses

OBVIOUS LOSSES

Most grieving is due to losses which are easy to identify. The source of grief is obvious when a person has lost a loved one, experienced divorce, moved away from friends, or lost or retired from a job. From your experience, list below some major losses which you can easily identify: _____

_____

_____

_____

_____

NOT-SO-OBVIOUS LOSSES

Many losses are difficult to identify, particularly because they may be associated with "happy" life changes. For example, loss may accompany graduation from college (loss of friends or loss of the somewhat carefree role of student). Exciting, positive events such as marriage or having a baby may also bring loss—loss of independence. Other common life experiences such as loss of health or loss of dreams may not be as easily acknowledged as the more obvious losses. Think back over your own life, and list some losses which you may not have been aware of as losses at the time they occurred:

_____

_____

LOSSES DUE TO AGE

Many losses occur because of age: the loss of childhood, youth, energy, independence, career, health, beauty, work. What losses have you experienced due to age?

_____

_____

_____

_____

LIMBO LOSSES

Some losses seem to just hang in limbo, losses which generate many of the same experiences as mourning an obvious loss. Examples of limbo losses are loss of trust, a dissolving partnership, a closing business, a missing person, an impending retirement, a loss of certainty or finality. What losses do you have "hanging in limbo"?

_____

_____

_____

_____

Note: These terms—obvious loss, not-so-obvious loss, loss due to age, and limbo loss—were introduced by Melba Colgrove, et al., in the book, *How To Survive The Loss of a Love.*[2]

Three Losses

As you review the **OBVIOUS LOSSES, NOT-SO-OBVIOUS LOSSES, LOSSES DUE TO AGE** and **LIMBO LOSSES**, choose three losses you have experienced which you would like to deal with throughout this book. You will refer to these losses as you progress.

LOSS #1 _____

_____

LOSS #2 _____

_____

LOSS #3 _____

_____

Classify each loss as obvious, not-so-obvious, a loss due to age, or a limbo loss.

Secondary Losses

As you focus on an obvious loss or major loss, you may fail to see the losses that surround the primary one. You may be mourning for the surrounding losses of which you are not aware.

◆ You are graduating from high school. You may be losing your friends and the familiar setting. That is your focused loss. However, you are probably also leaving your family and home, and you are losing your childhood, your nurturing community, familiarity, your lifestyle and a kind of carefree atmosphere.

◆ You have lost a spouse through divorce. You may focus on the loss of the mate, but you have probably lost a place to live, your role as a couple, your role as a wife or husband, your sense of identity, your social group and your dream of "forever together."

◆ You were not selected for the basketball team. It was your dream of a way to "make it" in high school. You saw yourself as a star when you played in junior high. Your focused loss is the place on the team, but you have also lost a dream, some prestige that you hoped for. Your self-esteem may also  have been damaged, and your parents may be disappointed, as well as your girlfriend or boyfriend. Perhaps your chance for a college scholarship is also lost.

◆ You realize that you are getting older, and suddenly it seems that you are not able to care for yourself anymore and must move to a place where there is more care for older people. You are focused on the loss of your home, but you have also lost your independence, your energy and stamina, your identity as a self-sufficient person, your neighbors, your space, things you have loved.

◆ Your job has been your life. Now it is time to retire. You have looked forward to this day with dread. You are focused on the loss of the job, but you may also be losing some self-esteem, your role, your prestige, the structure that goes with your day, your sense of worth.

◆ The boy you have dreamed about finally has arrived in your life. He has been a wonderful steady friend, but suddenly he starts going with the new girl in school and pays little attention to you. You have lost the boyfriend, but you have also lost the prestige that went with having a "steady," the security of having someone to go places with, the admiration of the other girls, the crowd that the two of you went out with.

◆ You have always liked having a "best friend." Suddenly, her parents get a divorce and she is moving away. You are losing a good friend, but you are also losing a person to call every night on the phone, someone who knows you and accepts you, someone to share homework with, a sense of self-esteem which comes with the security of always having someone available.

Our most painful experiences will often emerge as our most disguised teachers.

When you look at the totality of loss, you will always find many other losses which you have not considered as part of your grief. Unconsciously, you are mourning for these losses. It helps in understanding your grief to consider all the losses which you are experiencing.

As you look back at your three identified losses, what are some of the secondary losses which you may have experienced?

LOSS #1 _____

_____

_____

LOSS #2 _____

_____

_____

LOSS #3 _____

_____

_____

Review

As you look back at the last chapter, think of the area of greatest impact on you. What seemed to stay with you? What special impressions did you get? Fill out the following as related to this chapter.

I HAVE LEARNED/RELEARNED

_____

_____

_____

_____

_____

_____

I AM SURPRISED THAT

_____

_____

_____

_____

_____

_____

I REALIZED THAT

_____

_____

_____

_____

_____

_____

Chapter 2

How Do You React?

I do not believe that sheer suffering teaches. If suffering alone taught, all the world would be wise, since everyone suffers. To suffering must be added mourning, understanding, patience, love, openness, and the willingness to remain vulnerable.

◆   Anne Morrow-Lindbergh,
Hour of Gold, Hour of Lead [1]

Divorce: A Painful Life Change

When David was 12, he would wake in the night to hear his parents fighting. He was always frightened when he heard the yelling. It seemed that this always started softly as soon as his dad arrived home from work. Then it would escalate as the evening went on. When they thought he was asleep, they really let loose. One problem that was evident was his dad's late hours. His job was so unpredictable—he could never count on being home for supper.

David knew that his dad was working very hard to get the business started. He also knew that a lot of time had been spent in training, as his dad had gone to school for many years.

His mother had worked in a job until he was born, but she had not worked since. Many times she talked about how bored she was and that when he was older she might return to work. His dad made very good money so she did not have to earn a part of the income.

He could not sort out the exact cause of the problem. Maybe his mother just expected too much of his dad. Maybe his dad did work too much and put his work before the good of his family. Then again, Dad was working so that his family could have nice things. David was very confused.

Finally, one day his parents decided that they could not stay together. Dad came by and got his clothes and some personal things and moved out. David could not believe it when his dad said good-bye. He could not imagine Dad not coming home at night or living in another house. He did not want to live just with his mom. But Dad could not keep him because he was always at work.

David was very angry. He was angry at his mom for not understanding that Dad had to work hard. He was angry at his dad for working all the time and never having any time with them. He was angry at them both because they were destroying his life. He did not want to be torn between them. He did not want to live in two places. He did not want to be a "divorced" child. But David held his anger in; he did not want to scream as his parents did when they were angry. He wanted very much to stay in control of his emotions.

As he thought about the whole thing, he wondered if it was his fault. Maybe they would have made it had it not been necessary for his

mother to stay at home with him and for his dad to make so much money. Unfortunately, David did not discuss his fears with his mother or father. He had never heard his parents talk about feelings, so it never occurred to him to tell them how angry, guilty and confused he was.

At school David felt depressed. He could not study very well, and he got impatient with the teachers and the other students. It was hard to concentrate on his homework. Nobody seemed to understand. The first weekend when his dad came to get him, David felt very awkward. Dad's new house did not seem like home, even though David had a room of his own. He did not want a room in each house. He could not think of anything to say to Dad and wanted to go back home. When the weekend was over, he was relieved. But when he got back home, Mom was always nagging at him. She seemed very sad and impatient. It was gloomy in the evening when Dad did not come home and wrestle with him on the floor.

Soon David knew that it was really over. He began to give up his dream of getting his parents back together. David had a family, but now he had to adjust to a new kind of family. It was a tough experience.

Factors Which Affect Our Grieving Patterns

Grieving is highly individualized. No one can predict the time span for healing, the coping strategies and the manner in which grief is expressed. The intensity of our grief is often dependent on the significance of the person or thing lost. In David's case, as with most children of divorce, there was loss of the family that he had always known. Yes, he still had a mother and father, but they were no longer a unit. It was a big change for him, and he had lost his sense of security. Another child might react differently to his parents' divorce. If a boy had a distant, uncommunicative father, or was not accustomed to seeing him because he traveled a great deal, the loss might not seem as devastating.

How people respond to loss and how they grieve can be influenced by a number of factors:

FAMILY BACKGROUND
The modeling which you have observed from the adults around you who were experiencing grief set examples for you. If your family tended to be stoic, unemotional and apparently unmoved, you may find it harder to express emotion openly. The opposite may be true if you have witnessed much display of emotion— loud crying or screaming. You may respond in much the same manner as your family, or by deliberate effort you may express yourself differently.

◆ Marie's family was very demonstrative. They greeted guests with great gusto and made a celebration out of every holiday. When something was lost or was of great concern, they were just as demonstrative. They cried loudly, wailed, made even little things into big monsters. A death was an experience which Marie would never forget. She determined that she would never act like her family. She became stoic and unemotional. Like David, in the opening story of this chapter, she wanted to react differently from her family.

◆ Peter's family came from a reserved European background. They accepted life's experiences without fanfare. Even severe losses were dealt with in an unemotional way without any display of feelings. Peter's mother prided herself on not having cried in 25 years. No allowance was made for being "sissy." As a child and later as an adult, Peter found it very difficult to express his feelings.

FAMILY BACKGROUND

As you look at your family's reactions to losses, what do you see? _____

_____

_____

What example was set by your father? _____

_____

_____

What example was set by your mother? _____

_____

_____

What example was set by your brothers and sisters? _____

_____

_____

How do you model your pattern of mourning from these examples? _____

_____

_____

Grieve

For in the long run this may be the bravest thing to do.
Accept your feelings
Declare them when you choose
Give in to them for the moment
Appreciate them.

For sadness is a part of life.
In this expression, people can relate to you
And rejoice with you
In your humanness.

◆

Mary Joe Hannaford
Originally published, *APGA Journal*

CULTURE

Cultural patterns and customs will have a strong influence on your manner of expressing grief. The culture may model open expression or reserved, controlled grieving. Your community background will reflect the culture. You have been influenced by the way you have seen other people grieve around you. The strongest influence in handling loss will probably be built around the expressions made about death; however, you will observe reactions to divorce, natural disasters and more insignificant losses.

◆ In Adam's community almost everyone was of the same general cultural background. A "celebration" was held in time of great loss. For funerals there was even a parade down the street with a band playing. Many people came and stayed for days. The house was filled with good food, and everyone stood around and laughed and talked of good times. When the actual funeral took place, they dressed up and cried a lot. Adam was sometimes confused about the merriment and the sorrow being expressed at one time.

◆ In Ingrid's community only the immediate family was involved extensively in major losses such as death. The women always dressed in black, while the men wore black armbands. The period of mourning for the immediate family was a year, and during that time no one could sing, dance or show happiness in any way. The men would bear the body to the grave. At the funeral the living were always given an opportunity to express any concerns about having offended the deceased.

How does the culture in which you live influence you in developing your patterns of grieving? _____

_____

_____

_____

What are some local customs which may affect how you grieve?

_____

_____

_____

_____

What are some customs which you dislike and have tried to eliminate from your life? _____

_____

_____

_____

RELIGIOUS TRAINING
Religious background has a significant influence on grieving. Some religious groups encourage open expression, while others are restrained and sometimes guilt producing. Some groups are so stoic that they do not allow any expression of sadness and state simply that "this is God's will."

During the winter, keep the vision of spring in your heart.

◆

◆ Paul grew up attending a church where losses such as divorce were never discussed, but death was responded to in a caring manner. Much prayer was requested for the family faced with the impending death of a loved one and for the healing of the person. It was not considered necessary to have a minister present at the time of death, and there were no particular church rules about funerals, cremation or interment. Such decisions were largely up to the immediate family. Flowers and bearers of the casket were considered usual parts of the ceremony. Friends generally visited the family after the services.

◆ In Yon's church it was necessary for a minister to be present immediately after death. There was usually a wake prior to the funeral service. The family was free to select the manner of interment or cremation. In case of cremation, a memorial service might take place. Music was an important part of the service.

As you review the traditions of your religion, how does your religious training influence your patterns of grieving?

_____

_____

_____

_____

What lessons from your religious background do you value and use in the process of grieving? _____

_____

_____

_____

What lessons from this background that you see as harmful have you decided to eliminate from your patterns?

_____

_____

_____

_____

FAITH AND SPIRITUAL BELIEF

Your faith in God (or lack of faith) may be an extension of the ceremonies and rituals of your religious training. If you have not been introduced to the doctrine of a particular religion, however, you may have acquired certain spiritual beliefs through courses in school, through reading, or from associations with others who have a philosophy that appeals to you. Your belief about the hereafter, about your personal destiny, about an overall plan from a higher power or the belief that this life is all there is will determine much of your direction in working through loss.

◆ Sarah believes that everything in this life has a purpose. She is constantly aware of the presence of a higher power directing her daily activities. Therefore, when loss occurs she looks quickly for the learning which is taking place in her life and submits to the direction which she is taking. She believes there is a purpose for everything.

◆ Frank has accepted the teachings of his church that this life is all there is. He believes that we do good in this world in order to live on in the lives of others—in their memories. He does not accept the concept of life after death. He does believe that service to others is essential to the good life.

How does your faith (or lack of faith) determine your value system in sorting out your destiny? _____

_____

_____

How do you reconcile loss as fitting into the scheme of things?

_____

_____

Which of your beliefs brings you comfort? _____

_____

_____

Which of your beliefs disturbs you? _____

_____

_____

HEALTH

When you are feeling well, physically and emotionally strong, you may be better able to cope with grief than when you are tired or not healthy. You may expect too much when you are not feeling strong enough to "cope" in the usual manner. Examine your level of health as you look at your responses to losses. Your awareness of stress management may be an important factor in getting through a period of mourning. Being consistently aware of diet, exercise, play and humor, quiet time (meditation) and having a confidant or friend to talk with are resources of protection. Using artificial means of comfort such as alcohol or other drugs can be destructive to your progress.

◆ Susan had not been well since her surgery. She had hurried back to work in order to maintain her income. It seemed that she just couldn't get her strength back. Her boss retired just as she returned. He had been a good friend and supporter. Susan was disturbed about his leaving; then she got a call in the night that her mother had been taken to the hospital with a heart attack. Susan felt she couldn't handle anything else.

◆ Jess had broken his leg playing ball. Because he was in a cast for six weeks, Jess had missed the spring practice for the ball team. He felt left out of everything, was suffering discomfort from the break, and being confined had set him on edge. During that time Jess's dog ran out into the street and was hurt badly. Jess felt that he had just about come to the end. He overreacted to the dog's injury.

How do you see your health as contributing to the way you have reacted to loss? _____

_____

_____

What have you done to take special care of your health while you were grieving? _____

_____

_____

Support Systems

Loss seems easier to bear when you are surrounded by people who care about you. Their concern and support tend to give you increased strength. In some losses such as divorce, there are fewer support systems to call on than in more dramatic losses such as an

accident, a sudden death or a natural disaster. As you look back at the not-so-obvious losses, losses due to age or limbo losses, you may recall that support was conspicuously lacking. There were no cards, flowers, presents, or friends calling to offer comfort. In such cases it may be helpful to set up your own support program —through support groups in the

community, at hospitals or churches. You may want to ask people you trust to be available to you. They will likely be flattered that you have called on them to help with your healing.

◆ Jim was recently divorced. He had never thought he would be single again. It had been a rough time for him and his wife. Their only friends were couples whom they had known in college. Being alone was devastating to Jim. He felt uncomfortable talking with any of the couples, and nobody said much about the split-up. It was as if everyone avoided the subject. Of course, there were no cards, flowers or tangible gestures of caring. He felt very alone, but finally asked several friends for their support. He joined a group for singles at a local church.

◆ When Mary found out she had cancer, she was frightened and angry. It was her sophomore year in high school, and she had a lot of life that she wanted to live. When her friends at school found out, they did not know what to say and acted as if she had a contagious disease. They avoided her, and when they were with her they avoided the subject. Mary joined a support group for adolescents.

31

In the past, where have you found your greatest support in times of loss? _____

_____

_____

List nurturing support people to whom you would turn in times of loss. _____

_____

_____

As you look back at your losses, what did your friends do that was comforting? _____

_____

_____

_____

Knowledge and Understanding

Healing begins when we stop resisting the pain.

Although knowledge and understanding will not make grief less painful, understanding what is happening and knowing that the feelings are normal will make those feelings more bearable. Much fear and self-condemnation will be removed. Knowing the stages of grief will help you to understand that it is appropriate to feel those feelings and to pass through periods of gloom, doubt and guilt. Reading books about the grief experiences of others or comforting poetry and quotes can assure you that your grief is a normal part of the human experience.

◆ Virginia was overwhelmed when she was not accepted to medical school. She had always dreamed of being a doctor and had spent her undergraduate years taking the necessary science courses and getting experience which she thought would help. When the notice came, she was in shock. It was unbelievable to her. In a peer-helping course in college, Virginia had learned about the process of grieving. As she began to think about what was happening, she understood why she was angry, depressed and lonely, and was able to accept the progression toward healing. Her knowledge helped her to understand her feelings.

◆ Charles was very angry as he thought of the progressive illness of his daughter. Life was not fair in letting a little girl suffer. Charles resented his own helplessness and was unable to identify all the things that were happening. Because of his religious background, he was trying to be brave—putting on a good front for his church friends. He didn't want them to know that his faith was weakening. Charles was unable to accept his feelings as normal. His knowledge was so limited about the grief experience that he was unable to interpret what was happening to him.

What have you read or learned that helps you understand the grieving process? _____

_____

_____

_____

What workshops/meetings/seminars have you attended that helped you gain knowledge about handling loss? _____

_____

_____

_____

Somehow if we are at home within ourselves, we will be at peace as we change "homes."

◆

Personality

The way we grieve can be influenced by our personality. If you are extroverted and enjoy people, you may find it easier to reach out and express your feelings readily. But if you are quiet and withdrawn or shy, you may find it difficult to gather people around you or to express your inner thoughts.

How do you see your personality type influencing the way you grieve? _____

_____

_____

_____

What do you see as especially difficult for your personality type in times of crisis? _____

_____

_____

_____

As we identify our losses, weave through the pain, reflect upon their meaning and move into the healing, the fragments of our lives begin to come together and life begins to make sense again.

◆   Joyce Rupp,
Praying Our Goodbyes[3]

Reaction Patterns

Many of the influences in your life will affect your reactions to loss. It can be important to identify your usual first reactions, as well as succeeding responses, in knowing what expectations you have of yourself as you face future losses. What  were your first reactions to past losses? Try to recall exactly what you thought, felt and did when you experienced the loss. Then look for a pattern in your reactions.

REACTION PATTERNS FOR THREE LOSSES

Loss #1 _____

What was my first reaction? _____

What did I think? _____

What did I feel? _____

What did I do? _____

_____

_____

Loss #2 _____

What was my first reaction? _____

What did I think? _____

What did I feel? _____

What did I do? _____

_____

_____

Loss #3 _____

What was my first reaction? _____

What did I think? _____

What did I feel? _____

What did I do? _____

_____

_____

Stages of Grieving

Various stages of grieving are experienced as a result of loss. All the stages are not experienced by everyone, nor do they occur in a certain order. Understanding these stages will help you accept your feelings.

After each stage is described, refer back to the three losses you have listed. Try to think of times when you were experiencing that stage. Write that in the space provided.

SHOCK

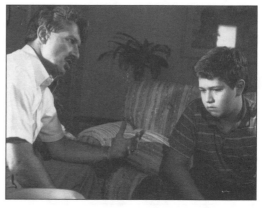

Initially, a loss produces a kind of anesthetized response which protects you from the impact of the blow. This experience can last momentarily or for several days or weeks depending on the impact of the blow and the readiness of the mind and body to move on. Shock sometimes provides enough anesthetic for a person to continue normal activities for awhile, make decisions and take care of immediate needs.

◆ Mildred was notified about her job loss after a merger of her company. All afternoon Mildred felt a kind of numbness but kept working in the usual manner. She was surprised at how many things she got done. It was as if nothing had happened. She really did not feel anything. Mildred was in shock. It was not until she got home that she realized she would not be going back to that office.

When have you experienced shock as a result of a loss? _____

_____

What did you think? _____

_____

What did you feel? _____

_____

How did you act? _____

_____

PANIC

As a grieving person, you may have a hard time concentrating. You may not be able to get your mind off the loss. Naturally this hinders your effectiveness. You feel that you are losing your mind and won't be able to function at all. This causes you to panic and become paralyzed with fear. Your real fear comes from not understanding the grief process in advance.

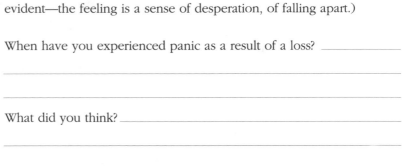

◆ Julie went outside to ride her bike. It was not in the place where she had left it a few minutes before. She ran screaming into the house. When her mother wanted to know what was wrong, she just kept screaming. She couldn't even think of what to say to her mother. Trying to speak or think was impossible. Tears ran down her cheeks as she tried to catch her breath. Julie was experiencing panic. (Sometimes panic is internalized so that no outward behavior is evident—the feeling is a sense of desperation, of falling apart.)

When have you experienced panic as a result of a loss? _____

_____

What did you think? _____

_____

_____

What did you feel? _____

_____

How did you act? _____

_____

DENIAL

It is often said that people who stubbornly refuse to grieve are "in denial." Grief is painful and they feel that it will be less painful not to accept or face the loss. This is not true, of course, since postponed grief only means that it will come later and take longer to resolve. People are denying their feelings when they say, "It really doesn't bother me." That is simply a way of saying, "I will not let it hurt." It takes great courage to grieve. Denial for a limited period is, however, normal and healthy. If it continues for months or years, it may be impossible for the person to complete the healing process.

◆ Sam was on schedule for the next selection of the basketball team captain. He knew that he had been a good player and was respected as a leader on the team. He awoke  anxiously the morning of the announcement, picturing the thrill he would experience when the other boys heard the news. When the coach called the team together, he announced that Bill would be the new captain. First, Sam experienced shock—he just couldn't believe this had happened. Then he felt it wasn't true. In trying to pull himself together, he told the boys who offered consolation that he really didn't want to be captain anyway. He told himself that his academic schedule was too full for him to take on the responsibility. Sam kept telling himself that he didn't care. Sam was experiencing denial.

When have you experienced denial as a result of a loss? _____

_____

What did you think? _____

_____

What did you feel? _____

_____

How did you act? _____

_____

RELEASE

As reality begins to dawn, emotional breakdown may come, tear glands may overflow, sobbing may come. Remember, tear glands are there to be used. Holding back may be a sign of trouble, rather than a symbol of bravery. To bottle up feelings unnecessarily may be harmful. Emotions may be released by talking, shouting, running or working. In whatever form they are expressed, they must be released.

◆ Louise was overwhelmed when she realized that her son had been using drugs. She had suspected that he was but had denied the possibility. The son she had hoped for would not do such a thing. When she finally realized that the news was true, she burst into tears. For days she had gone along feeling that she was handling the whole truth very calmly, but suddenly it hit. All afternoon Louise stayed busy, hurrying through her work so that she would not have time to think. Louise was releasing both with tears and with excessive work.

When have you experienced release? _____

_____

What did you think? _____

_____

_____

What did you feel? _____

_____

How did you act? _____

_____

GUILT

Feelings of guilt may emerge during the grieving process. You may be concerned about what you failed to do to avoid the loss. What did you not do to enhance the relationship? What did you do that hurt the other person? Normal guilt includes thinking of some things you didn't do, since no relationship is perfect. Neurotic guilt is out of proportion to the real involvement. Guilt left unresolved can cause long-standing misery and a variety of physical symptoms.

If you were actually guilty of neglect or a deliberate act which contributed to a loss, it is important to admit your involvement, ask for forgiveness from the parties involved and forgive yourself. Counseling may be in order so that you can move on with your life.

◆ Stephanie raced to the phone as soon as she found Richard on the floor. An ambulance came quickly and took him to the hospital. It seemed forever before they checked him in and a doctor saw him. He had a stroke which eventually took his life. Stephanie went through shock, panic and denial. She just knew that Richard would be all right. When he did not recover, she felt that she had been negligent. Why hadn't she paid more attention when he said he didn't feel well? Had she phoned for help soon enough? Why hadn't she put more pressure on the hospital staff to tend to him and get the doctor sooner? No matter what she did, she couldn't stop thinking that she should have functioned more efficiently. For months Stephanie was caught up in the idea that it was all her fault. Stephanie was overwhelmed with unrealistic guilt.

It is difficult for anyone going through a period of brokenness (loss), a time in the desert or wilderness, to believe that somewhere down the road, all will be well.

◆ Joyce Rupp,
Praying Our Goodbyes[4]

GUILT

When have you experienced guilt as a result of a loss? _____

_____

What did you think? _____

_____

What did you feel? _____

_____

How did you act? _____

_____

Have you experienced a loss for which you felt responsible? _____

_____

How did you handle your feelings of guilt? _____

_____

What did you do to forgive yourself? _____

_____

ANGER

As stronger emotions appear, you may be resentful or angry with the person who has died, or with the persons who were responsible for his or her care. Anger may be experienced at being let down or disappointed. In cases of divorce, the person has not only rejected you, but has destroyed your dream of home, family and togetherness. Anger at yourself may be experienced after a loss. Anger may even be felt toward God. The human mind often looks for somebody to blame. You may blame friends for lack of comfort and family for not giving enough care.

◆ Doris was overwhelmed when Tom was killed on the job, leaving her with five children. She had not worked since the children were born, and the insurance was minimal. In the period following the shock and panic which she felt so severely, she would wake in the night resenting the task which Tom had left her, resenting his carelessness in having an accident, angry that he had not made enough money to support them adequately, and angry with God for taking away the father of her children. Doris was experiencing normal anger that goes with the grieving process.

When have you experienced anger or resentment as a result of a loss? _____

_____

_____

What did you think? _____

_____

What did you feel? _____

_____

How did you act? _____

_____

DEPRESSION

No two people face grief in exactly the same way. But whatever the experience, most often it brings feelings of isolation and loneliness. The clouds seem to hang low and gray with no signs of sun breaking through. Thoughts that nobody cares or understands are not unusual. Even God seems far away or out of sight. One thing to remember is that clouds are moving, but they do not move smoothly. Some days it seems that they have moved away entirely, but they return unexpectedly and sometimes remain for days.

◆ Jamie was pleased and happy when her boyfriend gave her an engagement ring. She dreamed of a wonderful future together. When he arrived one evening, he told her that he had decided it was too soon to get tied down and he wanted to call it off. After going through shock and anger, with some guilt about what she might have done wrong, Jamie became depressed. The person she loved was gone, and the dreams she had for the future were over. The clouds were so dense, Jamie sometimes thought she could not function. Every morning she felt she was just pulling herself into the day. Nobody seemed to understand how serious this was for her. Jamie was depressed and lonely.

When have you experienced depression/loneliness/sadness as a result of a loss? _____

_____

What did you think? _____

_____

What did you feel? _____

_____

How did you act? _____

RETURNING

As the grieving process progresses, you may want your life to return to its usual pace but may resist the first steps. Other people will not understand your heavy heart. Everyone seems to have forgotten the tragedy but you. You are trying to keep the memory alive by not returning. You may feel guilty about giving up the grieving. But as you begin to gradually add activities to your schedule, you will find that you are returning to responsiveness—a positive movement toward healing.

◆ After Charlie's wife died, he was numb. The loneliness was overwhelming, and he felt that he never wanted to do anything again. He walked through each day, getting his work done in a routine fashion. Then a new project came up in his office, and he found that it excited him. Charlie realized that after months of not caring, he was beginning to enjoy a few things again. Charlie was returning from mourning.

When have you experienced a period of returning as a result of a loss?

_____

_____

What did you think? _____

_____

What did you feel? _____

_____

How did you act? _____

_____

HOPE

The clouds begin to break and the sun comes through. This does not mean that clouds will not return, but they will be less severe and pass more quickly when they do return. Length of grief varies from one person to another just as stages and severity vary. Even with major losses, for most people more sunlight shows through after the first anniversary passes.

 The divorce was devastating to Kim. She had really loved her husband even though they had disagreements. She couldn't believe she had been so trusting. On the day he left, she was in shock; later, she moved through anger and resentment, depression and loneliness, and then guilt. She felt that she had experienced the whole range of the grieving experience. Then she decided to take a trip with a group she knew. Nearly a year had passed, and she felt a kind of healing inside herself. She was excited about the trip and planned for it for more than a month. Kim was beginning to look to the future with hope.

When have you experienced hope as a result of a loss? _____

_____

_____

What did you think? _____

_____

What did you feel? _____

_____

How did you act? _____

_____

ACCEPTANCE

After an experience of loss, you will not return to your old self. As all of life's experiences provide change and growth, so does loss. You can, however, become a stronger, more feeling person by accepting and finding meaning in your loss experiences and by helping others face similar tragedies. Faith seems to be a major factor for many people in this growth towards health and wholeness. Persons who work

through their grief do not deny the pain of the experience or expect life to be the same again. They take up the pieces and make them useful.

◆ Mark was 15 when his father divorced his mother. Mark loved his father, even though he knew that his father had neglected his mother and him. He was very sad for a long time after the divorce, but somehow during that period he found himself listening to other students who had similar experiences. Mark found great comfort in this kind of support and decided to form a support group in his school for students who wanted to talk about dealing with divorce. The experience led Mark to his college major in psychology where he began to develop his dream of being a counselor. Mark took his own sadness and turned it into an area where he found great satisfaction.

I know I have healed when I can say, "I shall be richer all my life for having accepted this sorrow."

◆

When have you turned a loss into a learning experience? _____

_____

_____

What did you think? _____

_____

What did you feel? _____

_____

What did you do? _____

_____

Even if you have worked through the beginning stages of grief, you may not have had time to work your way to hope, returning and acceptance. Give yourself time to experience the necessary ingredients for healing, looking toward what you are learning from the experience and asking yourself the question—"How will this experience bring a richer meaning to my life?"

What do you think you are learning from this experience? _____

_____

_____

_____

How can the experience enrich your life? _____

_____

It is very important to remember that

◆ the stages are not experienced in a smooth order

◆ everybody does not experience every stage

◆ you may return to a stage over and over again

◆ understanding the stages helps you to accept the normality of the experience

Separation

I cut the cords that
Laced us together
One by one.
As we slip gently apart
The pain is hard to bear.
But as each recovery
Moves from step to step,
I take another move
Toward separation.

I cut the cords that
Laced us together
But hold to one
Remaining there.
You were so dear to me,
I shall forever hold tenaciously
To that last cord of Memory
And feel that you are
Always there.

Mary Joe Hannaford

Review

As you look back at the last chapter, think of the area of greatest impact on you. What seemed to stay with you? What special impressions did you get? Fill out the following as related to this chapter.

I HAVE LEARNED/RELEARNED

_____

_____

_____

_____

_____

I AM SURPRISED THAT

_____

_____

_____

_____

_____

I REALIZED THAT

_____

_____

_____

_____

_____

Chapter 3

How Do You Cope?

*The price of good-bye is always high, but we must have the strength
to say good-bye before we can experience the joy of saying hello.*

◆

Losing a Much-Loved Pet

*L*ouie arrived at the train station in a crate, his black eyes
eagerly investigating his new world. He had come from
Missouri to live with us in Atlanta. The railroad employees
admired him and complimented his patience as we paid
the shipping bill.

The lady who sold him to us had recommended his breed, but
regardless of his pedigree, the little black dog was a treasure to us
from the beginning. In fact, we were all very attached to him
before we ever reached home that day.

During Louie's first year, he experienced adventures that kept us
frightened and protective. One day he disappeared and was gone
for more than six hours. Frantic, we feared that he had been
kidnapped, and we soon discovered that he had been. Late in the
evening, when we had given up hope of ever seeing him again, we
heard a car in front of our house. We rushed out to see who it was,
but they were pulling away and Louie was wandering toward us.

Throughout his lifetime, Louie slept with us, ate with us and
traveled with us. He also provided us with lots of laughs. Once
when we left him at home alone, he took something from
everyone's bedroom and piled it all in the hall. We weren't sure
of the message, but we believed that Louie was making a
statement about being deserted!

Louie was truly a member of our family. On his birthdays we let
him eat at the table so that he could have ice cream and cake with
the rest of us. Of course, we helped him blow out the candles. At
Christmas we always gave him a stocking and presents, and he had
great fun ripping up the paper we'd removed from our packages.

At 17, Louie developed a kidney infection. We knew he was not feeling well because his eyes looked sad and he had no energy. He was very old for a dog, but we didn't want to face the fact that one day he would die. As he

grew more feeble, we took him to the veterinarian more often. Finally, the doctor said that he would try several treatments for one week. If those didn't work, we would have to decide what to do about Louie.

After four treatments Louie was no better. We were frightened. We held him and rocked him in the rocking chair, but he rolled his eyes weakly as if he were tired of living. He couldn't walk without our help.

On the day of Louie's last treatment, the doctor phoned to say that Louie had gone into shock and that we should come to his office. Our family arrived from different parts of the city and nearly filled the doctor's parking lot with our cars. We wanted to say good-bye to Louie, but we sensed that he had already died. When the doctor confirmed our fears, we all cried, and we asked to see Louie one last time.

The doctor kept Louie's body until we could dig a grave for him at our home. It was nearly dark when we got there, but we dug the grave in the backyard near a bed of azaleas where he had frequently played. That night the house seemed quiet and empty. Louie's toys, scattered around the house, were reminders of the good times we had enjoyed together.

After getting Louie's body from the doctor's office, we all gathered for a funeral; we each shared a memory about Louie, discussed what he had given us, and planted colorful flowers on his grave.

It's taken us a long time to get over missing Louie. He's been dead for over a year, but now and then I think of him and get another tear in my eye.

After reading this story, answer these questions:

What was the major loss? _____

_____

What was the first reaction? _____

_____

What happened next? _____

_____

_____

What other reactions did you notice? _____

_____

_____

_____

What was lost in addition to the dog? _____

_____

_____

_____

_____

What was gained from the experience? _____

_____

_____

_____

Coping Mechanisms

Every person works out some method of surviving or maintaining equilibrium during a time of crisis. For instance, taking long walks or turning to gardening may be ways of working out your own approach, something that works for you when the "chips are down." Healthy ways of coping will ultimately mean that you come out on top—you work your way toward productive living. Some healthy survival reactions are:

CRYING

A sudden burst into tears or a soft sobbing may be a healthy way of letting the dam break. Crying in appropriate places and with appropriate people can be very healing. Crying with somebody can often be more comforting than crying alone.

WORKING

Many people find great solace in working. You may be distracted while working so that the pain does not seem so intense.

EXERCISING

Any form of physical activity or sport can be a distraction and give relief to the body and the emotions. Choose the type of exercise that seems most appropriate to your physical and emotional needs. It may be good to avoid highly competitive sports which put you under excessive pressure. Walking is recommended because it not only provides an outlet for the body, but also provides time to commune with nature. Running provides great comfort for those who have developed that activity. A good, silent run can help the whole system become more balanced.

READING

Books of comfort can assist you in thinking out your position. Novels, mysteries and non-fiction can provide distraction and time to be still and quiet. Reading scripture or poetry may give meditative relief.

PRAYING/MEDITATING

Praying in a form learned early in life or in a newly acquired method can provide much peace. Meditation can bring comfort from a greater power and put you in touch with your higher self.

TALKING

One of the best resources for many people is to have a confidant, someone who knows good listening skills and is willing to give some time to your healing. Sometimes much of the pain can be relieved by simply talking about how it feels. If friends get tired of listening, consider a paid professional counselor to get you through the tough times.

FINDING HUMOR

In every crisis there are humorous things that happen or are said. Sometimes even hurtful things that are said can be funny when we look back. It is an important source of healing to watch for the comical moments.

KEEPING A JOURNAL

Writing in a diary is a way of expressing your feelings and observations privately. Keep a notebook to jot down your thoughts of despair and your moments of discovery. Rereading from days past can help you evaluate your progress.

RITUALIZING

Funerals and memorial services are a form of ritual, but you may have many private rituals which bring comfort, such as the way you celebrate holidays, giving flowers in memory of the loss, and following personal routines.

REMINISCING

Remembering moments of pleasure which you once shared with the lost person brings comfort. These times may also increase in impact when they are shared with someone who has similar memories.

ENJOYING MUSIC

Choosing music which gives peaceful, tranquil feelings, or enjoying the lift from more lively music can set a mood of healing. Some comfort may be experienced when listening to music that reminds you of particular experiences with the person you have lost.

JOINING A SUPPORT GROUP

People with similar losses can find great energy by sharing their experiences with each other. Building a satisfying support system is especially important in times of significant loss. It may be automatic with available friends, or it may need to be devised for that specific purpose. If you cannot find a formal group to meet your needs, build your own support team. Ask others to join you in your grieving experience.

It is not a sign of weakness to have a personal or professional support person or group. It is a sign of intelligence.

◆   Ruth McSwain

When Coping Mechanisms Become Destructive

All of these methods of surviving can be harmful, however, if they are used in excess. If you walk or run so much that you are destructive to your body, you have taken a potentially healthy mechanism and turned it into an unhealthy one. This is true if you talk too much, work too much or cry too much. Use the coping strategies in moderation.

Some destructive coping mechanisms which may add to the difficulty of working through grief:

DRINKING ALCOHOLIC BEVERAGES EXCESSIVELY, SMOKING EXCESSIVELY OR TAKING OTHER DRUGS

These addictive behaviors add to the problem instead of providing a solution.

EXTREMES IN EATING HABITS

Overeating may bring immediate comfort, but in the long run it will add unnecessary pounds that are hard to shed. Stay away from the refrigerator except for healthy foods and snacks. Undereating can also be destructive. A healthy diet will help in the recovery period. Limit your use of caffeine and sugar, as both can serve as immediate stimulants and delayed depressants.

ISOLATION

Although time alone in prayer and meditation can be helpful, isolating yourself so that there is no social contact may lead to self-pity and depression.

Think carefully of the survival mechanisms which seem to be effective for you. Add others which you believe work well.

My most effective coping (survival) mechanisms:

Loneliness is one of the biggest problems of grief. It is your problem and you have to solve it alone.

Elisabeth Kubler-Ross, *Death, The Final Stage of Growth*[1]

_____

_____

_____

_____

_____

_____

_____

_____

Destructive mechanisms which I try to avoid:

_____

_____

_____

_____

_____

My nurturing support people are (these may be family, co-workers, church friends, school friends, counselor, neighbors, organized support group): _____

_____

_____

_____

Beliefs I rely on: _____

_____

_____

Books or other resources I rely on: _____

_____

_____

_____

BE GOOD TO YOURSELF

Choose an activity which you find especially comforting. You may choose participating in a sport, reading, sunbathing, getting a facial or new hairstyle, having a massage, having lunch with a friend, going dancing, strolling in the woods, bird watching. . . .

ONE-LINERS

Some of the following "one-liners" can become resources to help you get through times that are particularly stressful. *Carefully* select and use the ones which comfort you, but don't allow them to keep you from facing a problem.

- This, too, will pass.
- Take one day at a time.
- In the end, it will all be okay.
- God will provide.
- Expect the unexpected.
- No pain, no gain.
- Make the most of each day.

- Be good to yourself.
- Life is a gift, never to be taken for granted.
- Give yourself some time.
- Life is what we make it.

Note: These One-Liners are written by Joyce Rupp, in the book *Praying Our Goodbyes.* [2]

As you review these "one-liners," which ones would you choose to help you get through your personal loss? _____

_____

_____

Which do you think you might use too often, so that they would become barriers or crutches or prolong your denial stage?

_____

_____

DISTORTIONS AND MISCONCEPTIONS ABOUT GRIEVING

Much of your grieving may be distorted and confused by getting "stuck" in one or more of the following misconceptions. You may need to go over these ideas to check out your own belief system. Are any of these beliefs preventing you from moving toward wholeness?

Check the misconceptions or distortions which you feel have prevented you from progressing in your mourning.

- ☐ I have received so much that I have no right to go on with a happy life.
- ☐ I have only myself to blame for this loss.
- ☐ I must be angry at myself, not at someone else.
- ☐ I don't deserve to be happy.
- ☐ If I love myself, it will be egotistical and conceited.
- ☐ All that really matters is *me*.
- ☐ Self-forgiveness is self-indulgence.

- [ ] This just proves that I am a born loser.
- [ ] I will bury forever many of my memories; they make me too angry or sad.
- [ ] If I reflect on my past, it will be like opening Pandora's box; I'll just quit thinking.
- [ ] If I talk about it, I will just get in trouble.
- [ ] I will avoid people because they say so many dumb things.
- [ ] My real thoughts and feelings would shock my friends.
- [ ] You can't really trust anyone.
- [ ] The person I lost was perfect in every way.
- [ ] Marriage is only a piece of paper; I'll just tear mine up.
- [ ] Love never lasts.
- [ ] You have to just play the game, because nobody is sincere.
- [ ] True love is the end of all suffering.
- [ ] If I had lived a good life, this would not have happened to me.
- [ ] I have to put up a good front.
- [ ] Perfect love is the only kind of real love.
- [ ] I do not need others; I'll go it alone.
- [ ] Love means doing whatever the other person wants.
- [ ] I'll get even if it's the last thing I do.
- [ ] Love is blind.
- [ ] No commitment can last a lifetime.
- [ ] This is the way I am and always will be.
- [ ] I just can't make a decision.
- [ ] I just don't have the will power; I can't.
- [ ] It's easier just to give in or give up.
- [ ] Where there's a will there's a way; you can do anything you really want to do.
- [ ] I continually have to prove myself.
- [ ] Life is one "damn thing" after another.
- [ ] Life is easier if you don't stop to think about it.
- [ ] Good people do not suffer; virtue always triumphs in the end.
- [ ] I'll always remember the good old days; things will never be good again.
- [ ] Failure is failure, and all failure is final.

- [ ] I'm too old to start now.
- [ ] Prayer is for the weak.
- [ ] I will be a nobody if I don't have someone to love.
- [ ] It is a terrible, undeserved catastrophe when things are not working out.
- [ ] I must continually remember the dangers.
- [ ] I cannot exist without someone strong to protect me.
- [ ] I do not believe that life is difficult.
- [ ] I do not believe that life can be fair.
- [ ] Why me, God?

Add other misconceptions or distortions which you may have thought of as you read through these suggestions: _____

_____

_____

_____

HEALING CAN COME MORE QUICKLY IF YOU WILL . . .

- Grieve now. Don't put it off until later.
- Be kind to yourself.
- Rely on some old comforting relationships.
- Anticipate life.
- Allow yourself to be depressed or angry.
- Eat healthy foods.
- Remember that healing is not smooth; expect regression.
- Reject addictive activities (drugs, alcohol, tobacco, over/undereating).
- Recognize the need to move on with life.
- Release the guilt.
- Recognize the beauty in sadness.
- Go at your own pace.
- Reinforce your growing strength.
- Accept the new page in your book.
- Develop new interests.
- Join an organized support group.

Indelible

Without intending,
We came together
Unknowing that
In a short period
Our lives would blend
To giving
Part of ourselves
To each other.

Now we leave
No longer able to
Remove the impact
Thus experienced.

You have become
A part of me
That I cannot erase.
What I carry now
Is there
Forever.

Mary Joe Hannaford,
The Joy of Sorrow

- Seek counseling.
- Develop a confidant.
- Enjoy alone time.
- Meditate.
- Acknowledge your freedom to choose.
- Pat yourself on the back.
- Appreciate the privilege of loving.
- Recognize your choices.
- Create new opportunities.
- Discover the growth that is taking place in you.
- Forgive yourself and the other person, remembering that we all do the best we can in the light of our knowledge and feelings at the time.

What are you doing at the present time to encourage healing? _____

_____

_____

_____

What are some additional ways you have planned to help yourself move forward? _____

_____

_____

_____

Unresolved Grief

Sometimes you will find that you are living with a loss which won't go away. This may occur when you have either refused to grieve or have postponed grieving for various reasons.

DENYING THE LOSS

If you don't get a promotion that you desperately want, but insist to everyone (including yourself) that "it doesn't matter," you may still experience grief. When you say, "There's no problem," or pretend that nothing has happened, you are denying that there has been a loss. This avoidance of the issue, however, simply delays the healing process.

Not recognizing secondary losses may also cause negative emotions to linger. For example, you may have counted on the raise that would accompany the promotion you wanted. So anger may go hand-in-hand with your disappointment. In order to heal, it is important to acknowledge, rather than deny, both the primary and secondary losses that you experience.

GEOGRAPHICAL SEPARATION
When you are geographically separated from the place where the loss occurred or from social supports that you need, you may not feel the loss in the same way and may refuse to grieve because you are "geographically" alone. You may not experience the real loss until you return to that place and find that the person/thing is not there.

PERCEPTION OF STRENGTH
If your background, religious training or the people around you impose on you the image of being strong, controlled or stoic, you may find it difficult to allow yourself to grieve in your own individualized manner. It is important to give yourself permission to experience the grief.

AMBIVALENCE
You may not grieve because the person/thing really did not mean to you what you think is expected. You may feel both love and hate at the same time, which confuses the focus of your grieving. You may think other people expect you to be devastated or sad, when in actuality you have no sense of significant loss. For example, if you lost a parent with whom you always had a poor relationship or who had been abusive, you may be torn between feeling that you *should* have loved the parent and the reality that you didn't. This conflict may make mourning difficult.

LACK OF IDENTIFICATION

When you have failed to identify the loss, you naturally are confused about the focus of grieving. For this reason, it is extremely important to go back to the concept of loss identification mentioned earlier.

LACK OF EGO STRENGTH

Sometimes due to ill health, past experiences or low self-esteem, you may feel unable to absorb the impact of the loss. Under these circumstances, you find it easier to deny the loss and refuse to grieve.

Think back over times when you have experienced a loss and seemingly denied the loss or refused to grieve. Which of the six reasons mentioned seem to make the grieving more difficult? _____

_____

_____

_____

What could you do to deal with this issue? _____

_____

_____

_____

Anniversary Grief

Grieving seems to intensify at the anniversary of the loss. There is a kind of reliving of the event:

◆ It was a week ago that the loss took place.

◆ One month ago we were together.

◆ Today is his/her birthday.

◆ We moved a year ago today.

◆ It has been one year since the accident.

You will feel the pangs of loss as these events are re-experienced. The first year seems to be the hardest. However, after the first anniversary of each loss, the mourning usually begins to dissipate.

There is nothing on this earth that I can hold onto forever.

You will know that you have healed when you look back with tenderness and remember the experience without intense pain, and when you are investing your emotional energy in moving on. Look again at your three losses. If you have passed an anniversary—one week, one month, one year—what feelings did you experience on that anniversary? Did you see yourself going through the stages of grief mentioned in Chapter 2 again?

Loss #1 _____

_____

_____

Loss #2 _____

_____

_____

Loss #3 _____

_____

_____

Residual Grief

Years after the grief work seems to be completed, a sudden rush of loneliness or sorrow may burst upon the scene. It may be triggered by something which another person says, empathy with another person's loss or seeing a reminder of the person/thing. This need to grieve again will usually be very brief. The pain may be intense but short-lived. You may say in surprise, "I just don't know what came over me; that was a long time ago." It is important for you to recognize that you may have residual grief, and allow yourself the experience. This may not happen again for years, and it may not happen again at all.

Think of a time when you grieved again after a long absence of such a feeling. What did you experience and what were the accompanying feelings? _____

_____

_____

_____

Accumulated Grief

We will discover a new tranquility when we decide to turn loose of our need to possess and control.

At some period in your life, you may experience several primary losses in short spans of time.

Example: Your grandmother may die within a month after your divorce in September as your daughter leaves for college. Because of the divorce, you were forced to move to another town to respond to a job opportunity. You have experienced four or five major losses in a period of three months. Your grieving for one loss may overlap your grieving for another, and it may seem almost too much to bear.

Take your time. Be aware of the accumulation. Be patient with yourself and especially good to yourself. Apply the basic rules of good stress management. Be aware of the impact on your body and your emotional system. Reduce the demands you make on yourself. Review the stages of grief and allow yourself to move back and forth until you enter a period of hope.

Think of a time when you may have accumulated a number of primary losses. What experiences did you accumulate and how did you handle the feelings? _____

_____

_____

_____

Review

As you look back at the last chapter, think of the area of greatest impact on you. What seemed to stay with you? What special impressions did you get? Fill out the following as related to this chapter.

I HAVE LEARNED/RELEARNED

_____

_____

_____

_____

_____

_____

I AM SURPRISED THAT

_____

_____

_____

_____

_____

_____

_____

I REALIZED THAT

Chapter 4

_____

_____

_____

_____

_____

_____

What Have You Learned?

It is very difficult to go on believing, trusting, and trying to live during times of great loss.

◆ 　　　　Walter Bruggeman

Lessons From Sister

*T*he phone by the bed rang at 2:30 a.m., an ominous sound in the night. Since the phone is on my husband's side of the bed, he answered as I tried to wrestle with reality. I knew something was wrong from the limited number of words he was saying. Then I heard him say, "Let me let you talk with Mary Joe."

It was my niece, my sister's oldest child. During my sixteenth year, I had stayed with my sister as she was awaiting that birth. That was more than 30 years ago. The daughter was now an adult with her own family. "Mother is dead," she said in a matter-of-fact manner. Mother (my sister) lived in New Orleans on a college campus. "Dad came home late last night from a speaking engagement and found her in a pool of blood on the downstairs bathroom floor. We don't know if she hemorrhaged or if there was foul play. We are all leaving our homes to go down there, but we won't know anything about arrangements until we get there."

My first response was, "Tell your dad that we have some extra space in the family cemetery. I would be pleased if he would bury her there with Mom and Dad. We'll stay in touch. Call us as soon as you know something."

I lay back down in the dark. A harsh stillness encompassed the room. What was there to say? Sister had visited us for a weekend just three months ago.

To think that she was dead seemed impossible. She had undergone knee surgery five months previously and had been thrilled with her slow but deliberate progress. Her continual and simple faith was always an inspiration. How could someone so trusting be the victim of foul play? We didn't say much. Somehow it seemed important to think out the next day. Since we had no real knowledge of the event or the arrangements, we realized that our lives would be caught at a standstill until we had some sense of direction. We had to decide what to do about our jobs. Whom should we call? When should we go?

On the following morning, I was leading a seminar for 17 people in the counseling profession. They came regularly on Wednesday mornings for professional training and experiential group counseling. Instead of going to their regular positions, they reported directly to the workshop about 8 a.m. from various communities surrounding a large metropolitan area. How would I get in touch with them to tell them not to come? Questions—dozens of questions kept going through my mind as I lay there in the dark. The most prevalent feeling kept coming back—how frightened she must have been! I felt the fear rippling through my body. Emotions coursed through my system like ocean waves. Sleep came intermittently.

By morning I had decided. We rose at the usual 6 a.m. alarm. "What are you going to do?" my husband asked. We listed the people who we thought should be called. The calls were few because we had such limited information. Somehow we knew it had been foul play, an experience new to our family. We called New Orleans—no answer. We called her children—no answer. For the moment we were out of touch and dependent on them to communicate with us.

"I am going to work," I answered. "I can't possibly stay here. I don't know how to notify anybody not to come, and it will be good for me to keep busy." "Then I'll do the same," my husband remarked. "I'll keep trying to make contact. Since you are tied up in the seminar, just stop and call me from time to time. I'll at least know how to find you."

Breakfast, dressing and the ride to work seemed eerily ordinary in view of the events of the night. The traffic on the interstate moved rapidly, as usual. The world had kept going. The events of the last few hours had an unreal quality. Had this been a dream? Nothing else seemed changed.

The seminar participants gathered with their usual enthusiasm. It was a group of warm, friendly people who cared a great deal about each other and who related comfortably in a group. We all took our places. I continued the session according to our plan, with group participation as free and open as ever. From time to time, I slipped out during the discussion to use the phone. No information was yet available. Finally, contact was made and we found out the truth. It was murder. An intruder had entered the house and stabbed her to death in the living room. It seemed evident that her body was dragged to the downstairs bathroom floor where her husband had found her.

There is life after grief. Newness comes slowly and painfully. Life can be repatterned. You can start over very gradually.

Walter Bruggeman

I returned to the seminar, listening as the discussion continued. As was our custom, we had a sharing roundup at the end of the seminar disclosing some experience that we'd had during the past week. I was last in the sharing line-up. When my turn came, I still felt quite "together." I opened my mouth. "My sister was killed last night. We do not know exactly what happened." My chin started to quiver and tears came to my eyes. The group sat quietly by in shock. No words were said. They looked at each other and back at me. The tears came from all around the room. I could not speak. We just cried together.

As we sat in speechless stillness, the bond drew us into each other's sorrow. I broke the silence. "Okay, gang, the workshop's over—time to go back to work." Nobody moved. After a few exchanges, we got up and began to hug each other. An aura of support filled the room. In these wordless moments, it seemed that the power of touch generated the comfort we needed. Gradually, we moved out of the room with reassurance.

I canceled the remainder of the day's schedule and returned home. My husband met me there and we made arrangements to leave for the funeral after calling a few close friends. We gathered our own children together to finalize plans for the trip. The eight-hour journey was filled with dread. How could I walk into that house where she had lived so long? So many times during the past few years I had promised to visit. This spring I was planning to carry out that promise. What had we said during her last visit with me? What had we not said? Had she been frightened before, and had we not heard her mention it?

We approached the house. As we would expect, the street was lined with cars; people who had come to express their condolences filled the house. As I entered, I could feel the tears coming. I grabbed hold of Sister's husband and we sobbed together. We then sat and went over the whole story. I think it was good that we talked about everything—the blood on the stairs, the evidence on her body, her fear and calls for help. Heartbreaking as it was, it seemed important to cover every detail. As the story hit the national wire services, friends called from everywhere.

 The funeral was very impersonal. I tuned out what the minister said and thought my own thoughts—sad thoughts—and tears flowed silently. We went to another city for the burial, the place where my parents were buried. There they were, my dad, my mom and now my sister. There had been four of us, now there was just me. A wave of loneliness engulfed me. An orphan, I thought. I never had entertained the idea that someday I would be an orphan. There was a strange sense of removal from roots that had seemed solid for so long. Present family—husband and children—could not replace those shared memories of the family of origin. Nobody now shared my memory of the Christmas when I got my bicycle, or my doll Patsy, or my dog Spot, who was killed in the street. They were lonely memories.

Friends came and went. We all started back to work and resumed our daily schedules. Later, people told me how well I had done— assuming that I had recovered two months later. My heart was broken. Many days I cried all the way home from work. We talked about it a lot at home. My husband was a patient listener, but how many times could he hear this over and over again? Support came on a continuing basis from professional peers who were also trained in counseling. A professional pastoral counselor became my mirror, reflecting the reality of my feelings and giving me permission to travel through the guilt, the loneliness and the anger —anger at the murderer and at God.

I have looked back many times to that moment at 2:30 a.m. Now I must tell you that my sister was adopted by my parents when she was 3 years old—10 years before my birth. My mother often told me the story of how my father had picked my sister up in his arms and said to my mother, "Josye, let's take her home with us." On the night of her murder, as I lay in the bed reviewing the events, I saw my mom and dad very clearly and heard my dad say, "Why, Josye, here she is home again with us."

The scars will never completely go away, but someday we will look back and discover that the wounds have healed.

Now you may say that the experience was a figment of my imagination, or simply a dream, or just a rerun of what my mother had said to me as a child about the adoption, or you may say that it was a spiritual experience. Whatever your interpretation, it is all right with me. All I know is that it was very comforting.

A little over a year later, I was asked to speak at a conference. I offered to do a workshop while I was there. They asked me to do it on grieving. The audience was made up of counselors and social workers. I did it with great joy. Since then I have led dozens of seminars, given luncheon speeches and led studies on the subject of grieving. I have worked with high school leaders in peer counseling training, been in churches and religious meetings, worked with professionals, including international chaplains. The grief work has long been completed. I have moved on, but somewhere in my heart there will always remain a tenderness which I will purposely hold on to forever.

Perhaps you have never experienced loss of a loved one through death. If you have, you know that finding out about the death can be a shock, even when the person has been ill for a long time. For me the shock seemed to be magnified by the knowledge that my sister's had been a violent death. But following the shock, and the many other feelings that accompanied the loss, I was able to find meaning in the experience.

This chapter focuses on the learning that can take place after a loss—be it loss of a person, thing or belief. Taking a critical look at lessons you have learned and wisdom you have gained throughout your stages of grieving can be an important part of healing.

In the depth of the hurt and pain, you will have a hard time thinking of the ultimate meaning which this experience has to your life. To be able to ask, "What have I learned from this event that has made my life richer and more meaningful?" takes much time and work. Allowing yourself to move through the stages of grief is important. However, as you approach hope and acceptance, you will look back with great surprise at the lessons you have been learning.

In a special way we are continually being born and dying in each moment.

Let's think back on the "Lessons From Sister" story first, before we consider how loss can bring meaning.

What was the primary loss in the story? _____

_____

Identify the secondary losses (other losses that surrounded the primary one). _____

_____

_____

What did you see as the first reaction? _____

_____

What stages of grief are identifiable in the story? _____

_____

_____

What kind of coping mechanism (survival strategy) was used? _____

_____

_____

_____

_____

Can you identify a search for meaning? _____

_____

_____

What learning experience was evident? _____

_____

_____

_____

Learning After a Loss

Though you may presently feel anger, bitterness and remorse, you will eventually move healthily into the period of enlightenment when you can honestly say, "I do not want to ever experience that again, but I must admit that I am grateful for the lesson; I know that it has made me a wiser person."

You may have simply learned things which you will not do again or at least not in the same way. You may have learned that there are many things in life over which you have no control. Your ability to empathize may have increased. You may find that you can now share grief without embarrassment. You have experienced the reality of loss and understand the whole process of mourning better. You have mellowed and are more gentle.

Once again, look at your three identified losses. If a loss is relatively recent, you are probably in one of the stages of grief we have mentioned. If you are feeling some hope and reality (acceptance), you have probably begun to sort out some of your learning experiences.

LOSS #1
How has this experience changed my life? _____

_____

How has it influenced my life purpose and belief system?

_____

_____

_____

_____

_____

What positive action have I taken or could I take as a result of this lesson? _____

_____

_____

LOSS #2
How has this experience changed my life? _____

_____

_____

How has it influenced my life purpose and belief system?

_____

_____

_____

_____

_____

What positive action have I taken or could I take as a result of this lesson? _____

_____

_____

LOSS #3
How has this experience changed my life? _____

_____

_____

_____

How has it influenced my life purpose and belief system?

_____

_____

_____

_____

What positive action have I taken or could I take as a result of this lesson? _____

_____

_____

As I look back at these three losses, I evaluate the present level of grief as:

LOSS #1 **Time elapsed since the loss**   **My level of pain is**
          _____ days   5 very painful
          _____ months   4 not so intense
          _____ years   3 bearable
                                          2 limited
                                          1 rapidly healing
                                          0 healed

LOSS #2 **Time elapsed since the loss**   **My level of pain is**
          _____ days   5 very painful
          _____ months   4 not so intense
          _____ years   3 bearable
                                          2 limited
                                          1 rapidly healing
                                          0 healed

LOSS #3 **Time elapsed since the loss**   **My level of pain is**
          _____ days   5 very painful
          _____ months   4 not so intense
          _____ years   3 bearable
                                          2 limited
                                          1 rapidly healing
                                          0 healed

POSSIBLE MEANINGS

I have learned . . .

- that I can love.
- that loving hurts.
- that I can survive.
- that healing occurs.
- that I have grown.
- that I can forgive.
- that I can forgive myself.
- that you taught me much.
- that I can open my space.
- that I like sharing my space.
- that I can be a receiver.
- that change is a necessary part of life.
- that I am grateful for many things you gave me.
- that I wouldn't miss you if you hadn't been so important to me.
- that I cannot control everything.
- that I can care.
- that I can become involved.
- that I need a significant other.
- that I can re-evaluate myself.
- that I can check out my behavior patterns.
- that a new page in my life is being written.
- that I will have to change.
- that I can start again.
- that I am a richer person.
- that I am wiser.
- that I have discovered a new level of courage.
- that I am more open.
- that love is for me.
- that I can start anew.
- that I can make new contacts on my own.
- that I can gain self-confidence.
- that I am basically a social being.
- that I can expand my world.
- that I can ask for support.
- that I can flow with the healing process.

- that I have the courage to allow myself to feel.
- that I can still enjoy a sunset.
- that I am different.
- that I have evolved.
- that I am stronger, more independent, more joyful, happier.
- that I'm learning to like the independence.
- that I have choices.
- that I can make choices.
- that you will always be an essential part of my life.
- that I must take the first step toward healing.
- that I am really never alone.
- the value and importance of the present.
- to fill my days in new ways.
- to understand.
- to look at relationships more seriously.
- to look at attitudes.
- to look at weakness as a possible strength.
- to be more in touch with my feelings.
- to express my feelings more clearly.
- to appreciate life more.
- to appreciate this disruption in my life as motivation to grow.
- to experiment with new life styles.
- to enjoy aloneness.
- to tap resources of courage.

HEALING

Grief work will someday be completed. It really will go away, but sadness will always remain. You will know the grief is over when you don't feel any intense anguish or pain when you are reminded of the person or thing that was lost, and when you can turn the investment of emotional energy toward someone or something else. When you can look back with tenderness and pleasant memories, you will be letting go, but the loss of that person or thing will always be a part of your history.

Always Remaining

Looking back
I see clouds hanging low
And breathe a sigh
That they have drifted on.
Leaving Sadness
Standing there alone
In hesitation
Always remaining.

Looking out
I see hope rising
Like the dawning of the sun
Renewing warmth
Of morning light
That shines through
Open windows
Always beginning.

◆

Mary Joe Hannaford
Originally published, *APGA Journal*, October 1982,
on the anniversary of her sister's death.

Review

As you look back at the last chapter, think of the area of greatest impact on you. What seemed to stay with you? What special impressions did you get? Fill out the following as related to this chapter.

I HAVE LEARNED/RELEARNED

_____

_____

_____

_____

_____

_____

I AM SURPRISED THAT

_____

_____

_____

_____

_____

_____

I REALIZED THAT

_____

_____

_____

_____

_____

_____

Part II

When You Want To Help

Introduction

Helping seems to come naturally. Someone falls down, we help her up. A child needs a drink of water, we get it. A handicapped person needs the door opened, we do it for him. We help with social concerns—the hungry, the homeless and the handicapped—both individually and in groups.

It makes us feel good to be helpers. We may feel useful, valued or "close" to the person or people we have helped. But all too often, we are not skilled at being good helpers. A friend has a sudden tragic loss; a loved one loses his job; a child is distressed because her best friend is moving away. We want to reach out and offer help or support, but we don't know how.

In Part I of this book, you learned to deal with personal loss. Part II focuses on helping others. We can become better helpers by applying the knowledge we have gained from our own experiences, by learning to be more effective communicators and by understanding the stages of grieving that many people go through following a loss.

This section includes six steps which you may take toward becoming a more effective helper:

       Step 1. Be available.

       Step 2. Communicate caring and concern.

       Step 3. Support through the stages of grief.

       Step 4. Encourage healthy coping skills.

       Step 5. Help with a plan of action.

       Step 6. Guide toward finding meaning.

The first two steps address a situation which we must all face at some time: a neighbor, a co-worker or an acquaintance has had a loss. "How can I help?" you may wonder. Simply letting that person know you are available for them, and that you are concerned, can be helpful. When the person is not a close friend or relative, this may be all that you wish to do. On the other hand, if the person is important in your life, you may want to offer support throughout the grieving process. Steps 3 through 6 will assist you in doing that.

We are always in need of more healing, but someday as we walk through those moments, we will look back and know that we have walked out of the shadow.

◆

Chapter 1

Step 1
Be Available

We become healers when our own wounds become the major
source of our own healing power.

◆

Helping another handle loss requires a willingness to be there—both physically and emotionally. Being physically available means making the time to be with the person, making a commitment to offer our help. It means "going to the trouble" for someone else.

Being emotionally available means opening our hearts and minds in ways that may be painful to us, too. When we allow ourselves to "see with their eyes, hear with their ears, and feel with their hearts," as the psychiatrist Alfred Adler once said, we are truly positioned to be effective helpers. This takes emotional strength and energy. But being available enriches our lives as well as the lives of those we help.

Recognizing When Others Need Help

Losses such as death of a family member, divorce, major illness, job loss, natural disaster, fire or theft are obvious losses that are easy to recognize. Many people will rush to the person who experiences this kind of loss. As noted in Part I, it is the not-so-obvious losses that are somehow never shared or noticed. Some health losses, sometimes divorce, failure of a test, loss of dreams, even the loss of a pet may not be mentioned by anyone, yet the grief which follows can be devastating.

It is important for us as helpers to be able to recognize symptoms of loss. Tuning in to the feelings of the other person is the key. Facial expressions, tone of voice and body language are all clues to what is going on inside. When we can learn to recognize the pain and hurt in others without them having to tell us in words, we are in the best position to help. Look for signs such as the following:

- General sad appearance
- Extremes of gaiety
- Extremes of anger
- Abruptness
- Evasiveness
- Withdrawal

- Excessive laughing
- Dejected manner
- Lack of motivation
- Lack of interest
- Excessive aloneness
- Excessive sociability
- General fatigue
- Excessive working
- Drop in productivity or grades
- Unwillingness to be close
- Extreme dependency

Getting in Touch With Feelings

No one cares how much you know until they know how much you care.

To be an effective helper, be aware of your own feelings about loss and accept them.

Some people avoid or deny feelings that cause them discomfort, and they are probably not likely to reach out to someone else who is in pain. But individuals who are comfortable experiencing their emotions—from anger to elation—seem better equipped to help others through grief.

Example: **An effective helper**

Margaret was from a warm, affectionate family. When she learned that her neighbor had cancer, she quickly went to the neighbor's home and sat down to talk. With empathy she reached over to take her friend's hand and share her pain. Margaret felt the fear, the panic and the aloneness. She was not afraid of her own feelings, which gave her the freedom to share the feelings of the neighbor.

Example: **An ineffective helper**

Ben was raised by parents who did not show affection or permit expression of feelings. Their attitude was stoic, and they advised Ben that he should "take everything in stride." When his best friend in college did not get into medical school, the friend was shattered. Ben, however, did not know what to say. He wanted to be comforting, but he did not want to share the pain. He had no idea how to help, so he just left the room.

Think about your own family background. How did your parents express emotions? _____

_____

As you were growing up, how were you encouraged to discuss your feelings? _____

_____

What is your approach now? Do you openly discuss emotional issues—fears, expectations, disappointments, hopes—with your friends and family? _____

_____

_____

How do you feel about listening to others when they talk about their emotions? _____

_____

How would you rate yourself as a feeling person?

1	2	3	4	5

Avoid expressing emotions; deny need to process feelings

Express emotions freely; am comfortable with feelings

How does the way you rated yourself affect the way you deal with the feelings of others? _____

_____

_____

You may find it difficult to listen to other people express their feelings. To be an effective helper, you may want to expand your capacity to express your own feelings and to listen as others express theirs. Keeping two things in mind may help:

1. When feelings are not expressed, healing can be delayed or may be blocked indefinitely.
2. The ability to express a free range of emotions is a sign of strength, not weakness.

Ways We Avoid Helping

Regardless of how in touch we are with our feelings, most of us at one time or another have avoided reaching out to someone who is in pain. Think back as you read the following list. Have you ever used these methods to avoid helping someone who was grieving?

- ◆ Refused to look or listen
- ◆ Tuned out
- ◆ Refused to deal with your own pain
- ◆ Refused to feel the other person's pain
- ◆ Been unable to express feelings
- ◆ Seen only the person's pain, not the person as a whole
- ◆ Allowed the other person to become overly dependent
- ◆ Pushed the healing process too fast
- ◆ Made judgments about what the person should do or feel
- ◆ Believed that grief is a short term process

Perhaps you said to yourself:

- ■ I have enough problems of my own.
- ■ She could have prevented this if she'd tried.
- ■ I shouldn't help unless he asks.
- ■ It's really none of my business.
- ■ God helps those who help themselves.
- ■ If I get close, it may hurt too much.
- ■ If I help, will I ever get away?
- ■ What do I have to offer that's useful?
- ■ Is this problem too heavy for me to handle?
- ■ Do I have what it takes?

It is important in a world where everyone experiences the pain of loss to reach out to others. We can do this by accepting our own feelings; then we will be able to accept others' grief and not feel threatened. When we find ourselves making excuses not to help, such as those listed on the previous page, we can resist the temptation to avoid people with problems.

What ways have you used to avoid helping in the past? _____

_____

_____

_____

Have you ever felt that people were unwilling to help you? _____

_____

Describe how you felt. _____

_____

_____

Most people don't avoid helping because they are cold, uncaring or unfeeling; often they just don't know what to say or do, or they aren't comfortable dealing with unpleasant feelings. After taking a kind of "personal inventory"—by understanding our feelings and looking at how we avoid helping—we may make a conscious effort to be more empathetic and supportive when someone we know suffers a loss. Once we decide to reach out and "be available," we will want to let the person know that we care.

> *"What's a purpose?" Freddie had asked. "A reason for being,"*
> *Daniel had answered. "To make things more pleasant*
> *for others is a reason for being."*
>
> . . . .
>
> *"Each of us is different. We have had different experiences. We*
> *have faced the sun differently. We have cast shade differently."*
>
> ◆ Leo Buscaglia,
> *The Fall of Freddie The Leaf* [1]

Chapter 2

Step 2
Communicate
Caring and Concern

We give most of ourselves when we give gifts of the heart: love, kindness, joy, understanding, sympathy, tolerance, forgiveness.

◆   W.A. Peterson

When a friend or acquaintance has experienced a loss, how often have you thought, "I don't know what to say," or "I don't know what to do"?

Communicating our concern can be difficult. We don't know how the other person is feeling, so we can't simply say, "I know how you feel." We get caught up in worrying about saying or doing "the right thing," sometimes to the extent that we do nothing. One young woman whose mother died suddenly of a heart attack was hurt because a long-time friend never called or wrote to extend her sympathy. Years later, the friend confessed that she'd read about the death in the newspaper but did not know how to communicate her feelings. Consequently, she never reached out and told the young woman how she felt about the loss.

Many of us can relate to this story. When a person we care about is touched by tragedy, we are often perplexed about how we can help. We know the person is fragile and vulnerable, and we don't want to say or do anything to make matters worse. This chapter deals with the most important aspect of helping others through loss: communicating. It suggests simple ways to extend sympathy; but for those who wish to provide ongoing support through the grieving process, it also focuses on improving communication skills. Being an effective communicator is certainly important in all areas of life, but it is essential if we want to help someone who is in pain following a loss.

Expressions of Caring

We can communicate our sympathy to friends and loved ones in simple ways—by sending flowers, a gift, a sympathy card or personal note. We can offer to help—by caring for children, running errands or preparing food for the family.

Not everyone is good with words. We may know how we feel but find it difficult to convey our feelings in writing. Card shops are filled with beautifully written and illustrated messages of sympathy and caring. We can read through these to find one that expresses our concern and sorrow.

If you feel comfortable writing a personal message, try not to "block" yourself by analyzing how your words will be received. Instead, write from your heart. Tell the person exactly how you feel. "I was distressed to hear of the death of your mother. She was always so wonderful to me when we were growing up. . . ." If you have suffered a loss, think back about how others comforted you. Perhaps someone sent you a poem that you found helpful, and you saved it. Why not share it with the person you would like to console?

In deciding how you want to communicate your concern about someone's loss, here are some questions you can ask yourself:

What gifts are usually given to help comfort a person after a loss? _____

_____

_____

_____

_____

_____

What are additional ways I might express caring? _____

_____

_____

_____

_____

What are some thoughts I could write on a sympathy card? _____

_____

_____

_____

_____

_____

_____

What condolences did I find comforting after a loss? Which provided me the most comfort? Check the ones you would want to use to console someone else. _____

_____

_____

_____

_____

_____

What should *not* be said or done when offering consolation? _____

_____

_____

_____

_____

_____

What did others do for me to help me through a loss? _____

_____

_____

_____

What have I done for someone else that was effective? _____

_____

_____

_____

What were some things done for me in good intention that made my grieving more difficult? _____

_____

_____

What have I done for someone else that, looking back, was ineffective or inappropriate? _____

_____

When the person who has experienced a loss is a close friend, a co-worker whom we care about or a loved one, we often want to offer him more than a simple message or gesture of sympathy. We want to help him through the grieving process with love and support. The most effective way for us to do this is to acknowledge his loss, really listen as he talks about feelings, and let him know we're there for him.

Unfortunately, most of us are not very good communicators. We often hear what we want to hear, or worse, we don't listen at all. Sometimes we think offering advice or telling people how they should feel is communicating. Many times we fail to receive information that others send out non-verbally—through body posture, gestures and tone of voice. Building our communication skills will make us better helpers.

When we don't know what to do, all we have to do is listen, really listen.

◆

Effective Communication: Active Listening

When people fail to communicate effectively, the problem often lies with their listening. When we listen passively or with "half an ear," we miss too much vital information to be effective helpers.

Active listening means that we listen fully—not just with both ears, but with our eyes and intuition as well. We give the speaker 100 percent of our attention. We are fully available—physically and emotionally.

Active listening is a process of listening and responding, not just to the content of what is being said, but to the feelings that are often unsaid. When we listen to a person this way—"heart to heart"—the person feels cared for. That caring itself is healing. What is more, until the person who has lost feels that you do genuinely care about his feelings, the door to communication will not open more than a crack.

There are three parts to using active listening to communicate concern and caring:

    1. **Opening the door**
    2. **Listening and responding to feelings**
    3. **Avoiding communication blocks**

OPENING THE DOOR

We begin by letting the person who has lost know that we are available for support (Step 1). We can use words that will open the door to further communication as we are expressing our concern. As you look down this list of "door opening" statements, remember that what you say will be communicated more by your tone of voice and facial expression than by the words themselves. Your body language is also a powerful communicator. Leaning forward, moving toward the person, touching an arm or shoulder can all send a message of caring. When the other person is talking, verbal responses such as "um-hmm," "yes," or "I see" can let the person know you are with him.

- I have heard about your loss, and I want you to know that I care.

- It must be tough for you right now.

- I have been thinking about you.

- I want you to know that I am here for you.

- I feel your pain.

- Losing a _____ is a difficult experience. Remember, we all care about you.

- Please be aware that you have a lot of support from us all.

- I am available to you when you need me.

- You are not alone in this struggle.

List some other comments which you believe would acknowledge the loss and offer comfort. _____

_____

_____

_____

_____

_____

_____

With losses that are not so obvious, it may be harder to reach out to the person with offers of help. Here are some possibilities:

◆ I am concerned about you.

◆ I have noticed lately that you seem very tired. Would you like to talk about it?

◆ You seem upset about something. Would you like to borrow my ear?

◆ You seem to be working very hard lately; is everything all right?

◆ I really miss you; you seem preoccupied with something.

◆ Whatever is distracting you must be very important.

◆ Please know that I have a listening ear whenever you want to talk about it.

List some other comments that you think might successfully open doors of communication about a not-so-obvious loss.

_____

_____

_____

_____

_____

_____

LISTENING AND RESPONDING TO FEELINGS

Listening and responding to feelings are perhaps the two most important aspects of effective communication. In fact, the two are really interconnected. What we call "active listening" includes responding; as we have said, it is very different from "passive listening."

If you passively listen to a grieving person, you let her talk on and on without interacting with her. But if you listen actively, you participate and become involved in what is being said. Active listening is a skill; it requires practice. Your ability to listen actively will depend on

- your mood
- your feelings about the person
- your opinion about what is being said
- your own value system
- your beliefs about the event (the loss)
- your perception of your role as a helper

Listening actively means recognizing what the person is feeling, then responding by reflecting this feeling back to the person in words. You become what the late psychologist Haim Ginott called an "emotional mirror." The mirror's job is not to judge, criticize or interpret what it sees, only to reflect. By helping the person clarify her feelings and put them into words, you show that you are genuinely hearing what she says—not just the content, but the feelings beneath the content. Knowing that someone else understands and cares about what we are feeling deep down inside is comforting and healing.

Examples:

An effective helper

Griever: It is really a gloomy day.
Helper: It sounds like you're feeling bad about. . . .

An ineffective helper

Griever: It is really a gloomy day.
Helper: Some days are just like that. The sun will shine again.

An effective helper

Griever: Every time I think of him, I get mad.
Helper: You are very angry that. . . .

An ineffective helper

Griever: Every time I think of him, I get mad.
Helper: You shouldn't feel that way. He has his rights, too.

An effective helper

Griever: I just feel so left out of it all.
Helper: You are experiencing a lot of hurt because. . . .

An ineffective helper

Griever: I just feel so left out of it all.
Helper: You'll feel better tomorrow when you find something else to do.

An effective helper

Griever: I don't know what to do or where to turn.
Helper: You feel helpless because. . . .

An ineffective helper

Griever: I don't know what to do or where to turn.
Helper: Well, the first thing you ought to do is. . . .

You can vary the reflections by using phrases like:

◆ I wonder if you may be feeling. . . .

◆ Is it possible that you are feeling. . . .

◆ What I hear you saying is. . . .

◆ I get the impression that you are feeling. . . .

◆ It sounds like. . . .

Be sure that you are only checking out the feeling—not *telling* the person how he feels. You are verifying, not probing.

Expanding your feeling vocabulary will increase your skills as an active listener. Knowing some of these words may also prevent you from getting caught with limited responding words.

MILD	MODERATE	INTENSE
upset	fed up mad infuriated	angry irate
blue	down sorrowful gloomy	dejected depressed
concerned	scared afraid	terrified horrified
edgy	jittery nervous uptight	out of control
impatient	distrustful frustrated	disgusted
tired	weary listless fatigued	exhausted
sorry	disturbed regretful	guilty
hesitant	reluctant skeptical	turned-off
good	cheerful happy	elated thrilled
fondness	warm affectionate	loved idolized
O.K. confident	capable positive	on top of the world
safe	protected	secure
active	energetic enlivened	invigorated
calm	contented	brave at peace

What are some other feeling words that you would be comfortable using? _____

_____

_____

The following examples give you a chance to practice identifying feelings and then making an active listening response:

"I cannot live without her."

The most obvious feeling is _____

_____

Possible response: _____

_____

"It was all my fault."

The most obvious feeling is _____

_____

Possible response: _____

"If I had only come sooner."

The most obvious feeling is _____

_____

Possible response: _____

_____

"I knew this would happen."

The most obvious feeling is _____

_____

Possible response: _____

_____

"There is nothing left in my life now."

The most obvious feeling is _____

_____

Possible response: _____

_____

"I made it, so what?"

The most obvious feeling is _____

_____

Possible response: _____

_____

"I keep feeling so tired."

The most obvious feeling is _____

_____

Possible response: _____

_____

"Why would God allow this to happen?"

The most obvious feeling is _____

_____

Possible response: _____

_____

"I've always been a good person; I don't deserve this."

The most obvious feeling is _____

_____

Possible response: _____

_____

"I just can't figure out what life is all about."

The most obvious feeling is _____

_____

Possible response: _____

_____

"How could she do this to me?"

The most obvious feeling is _____

_____

Possible response: _____

_____

"It was my favorite thing in my whole life."

The most obvious feeling is _____

_____

Possible response: _____

_____

"Everything is gone—everything."

The most obvious feeling is _____

_____

Possible response: _____

_____

"It isn't fair—nothing is fair."

The most obvious feeling is _____

_____

Possible response: _____

_____

"I can't see the end—this will go on forever."

The most obvious feeling is _____

_____

Possible response: _____

_____

Check over your possible responses. Does each response reflect a feeling rather than a fact? Are any of the responses judgmental? Have you avoided giving advice such as "you should, you must, you have to, you ought to"?

TRY TO AVOID THESE COMMON ERRORS IN ACTIVE LISTENING:

- Overshooting and exaggerating the feeling

- Minimizing the feeling

- Adding to the feeling beyond what has been said

- Lagging or going back over old material

- Omitting or ignoring material

- Repeating the facts and not hearing the real message

- Analyzing or going beyond what was intended in the message

- Parroting what the speaker said, that is, repeating it back word for word

NON-VERBAL COMMUNICATION

The communication process is non-verbal as well as verbal. Behavior may express meaning more clearly than words. To be an effective communicator, focus on body language and tone of voice. Remember these points:

◆ Most of what we communicate is through *body language*.

◆ Some of what we communicate is through *tone of voice*.

◆ Very little of what we communicate is through *words*.

◆ *How* it's said is frequently more important than *what* is said.

In evaluating your own non-verbal communication skills, consider the following:

	DO	DON'T
Eyes	Give good eye contact	Stare, glare, avoid eye contact
Voice—Volume	Speak loudly enough to be heard clearly	Speak too softly or too loudly
Voice—Tone	Communicate in a tone of understanding	Sound disinterested, gruff, impatient, sarcastic
Facial expressions	Reflect your own or other's feelings	Frown, yawn, sigh, scowl, look blank
Posture	Lean forward slightly, relaxed	Lean away, be rigid, slouch, cross arms
Movement	Move toward	Move away
Distance	Position at arm's length	Position too closely (less than two feet); too far (more than five feet)
*Touch	Give handshakes, hugs (shoulder touch is usually acceptable, welcomed)	Grab, be overly affectionate

* Although touch is a great healer, it's best to use it with discretion; some individuals have had negative touch experiences, while others are simply not comfortable with touch.

AVOID COMMUNICATION BLOCKS

To truly help someone who has experienced a loss, it is important not to block communication by making statements or comments that would close the person off. For example, if the griever says, "I am very sad or lonely," you would want to avoid making these kinds of remarks:

1. **Threatening.** "Feeling like that will only make things worse."

2. **Lecturing.** "You should be glad—it could have been so much worse."

3. **Moralizing.** "You ought to be trying harder."

4. **Blaming.** "Well, maybe you brought this on yourself."

5. **Advising.** "If I were you, I'd start getting out more."

6. **Oversympathizing.** "It's too bad that so many terrible things happen to you."

7. **Questioning as probing.** "Well, what is making you so sad?"

8. **Kidding.** "I never would have guessed it. You don't look sad to me."

9. **Sarcasm.** "Well, how can a sweet thing like you be sad?"

10. **Praising.** "You really are great, you have so much to be thankful for."

11. **Name-calling.** "Big boys don't cry—cheer up."

12. **Ordering/commanding.** "Don't give me that stuff—get up and get busy."

13. **Criticizing.** "Feeling like that won't get you anywhere."

14. **Analyzing.** "You're just feeling inferior today—you'll work it out when you see how lucky you've been."

15. **Rejecting.** "It's up to you. I can't do anything about it."

16. **Counterattack.** "Well, look at how many other people are more sad than you."

17. **Placating.** "Well, everybody feels sad and lonely some of the time."

18. **Overidentifying.** "I know what you mean. I have been really sad all this week."

Do not decide on the outcome. The outcome is not within our power. The helping is now within the discovery.

When you assume these roles or respond in this manner, you do not allow the griever the right to experience her own pain and grow toward wholeness. The griever experiences this as a form of disrespect and backs away from the deep sharing that would help heal. Communication becomes either polite or superficial, or is altogether blocked.

Using active listening to communicate your concern and caring is a skill. Like any new skill, it will seem awkward at first. Do not worry about doing it perfectly. If you will continue to practice listening actively, you will find that it becomes more and more natural.

DOs AND DON'Ts FOR HELPERS

Consider these dos and don'ts when you want to express your feelings or reach out to a loved one or friend who has experienced a loss.

DOs:

DO communicate genuine caring. This will be done through your body language, tone of voice, and the words you say. By just being present, you will strongly express your concern.

DO be available to listen and to help in whatever way seems needed at the time— running an errand, making a necessary telephone call, accompanying the griever to a place where he needs to go. Be careful, however, not to do those activities that the griever can or wants to do on his own. Feeling helpless can be depressing.

DO express your concern about what has happened and acknowledge the griever's pain. Saying that you recognize the hurt can be very comforting.

DO remember the children involved. Somehow adults tend to get caught up in their own grief and forget that children also hurt. Children may not only hurt, but they may also be confused and in need of attention. It is hard for children to comprehend loss and recovery.

DO reassure the griever that he is not responsible for the loss. Even if some responsibility is his, remind him that he did the best he could at the moment.

DO encourage the griever to express her feelings in her own way—when she needs and wants to. A good cry while you stand by can be healing for some people. Shared tears seem to be more healing than tears cried alone. Sometimes holding a person's hand, or even holding her while she cries, is both appropriate and comforting.

DO encourage the use of survival skills. Reinforce the use of activities that provide the person the greatest comfort.

DO tune in to the feelings. "You must find this very painful, frustrating, upsetting, embarrassing, tough, difficult." (Select one response.)

DO acknowledge the other person's immediate need.

> "You are having a difficult time right now."
> "You are hurting where you are now."
> "It's tough, isn't it?"
> "Could we get together for dinner and just talk?"

DON'Ts:

DON'T let your own sense of helplessness keep you from reaching out to a grieving person. You may wonder what you can do. One of the most important things to do is to *be present*, both physically and emotionally.

DON'T avoid the griever because you are uncomfortable. Many times you may be unsure about what to say. Again, remember that being present may be more important than saying anything. It is lonely to experience loss when everyone seems to be ignoring your pain. You may also avoid communication because you think that mentioning the loss will make the person cry. Remember that tears are healing and the person is already sad. Opening that door may be helpful.

DON'T give the griever a time line about the termination of his grief. "You ought to feel better by now" will make the person feel worse. Remember that the period of grieving is dependent on the significance of the loss to the griever. You cannot rank the significance of that loss.

DON'T tell the person how she should feel or what she should do. It is important that you communicate acceptance of the place where the griever is and that you give her space to make decisions.

DON'T try to find something positive such as a moral lesson, or remind the person of the good things that are left or what he has to be thankful for. *Don't* remind the griever that at least he has other people or that he can always "get another one." Moralizing will break communication and produce feelings of guilt.

DON'T mention in any way that the griever might have been negligent or that the care of other people (doctors, hospital, teachers, friends) might have been misdirected. Even though this may be true, this is not the time for the hurting person to have to deal with these thoughts.

DON'T say that this is God's will. You may be tampering with the person's faith in God, which can sustain.

DON'T say that you know how he feels. It is difficult to know how another person feels even when you have had a similar loss. However, it is appropriate to compare losses. It may be comforting to the person to know that you have had a similar experience.

Add any other areas to avoid which you have discovered.

_____

_____

_____

The recommendations for effective communications in this chapter require practice. Simply reading about them once or twice will not make you a better helper. Don't be surprised to catch yourself doing one of the DON'Ts in everyday situations—like telling someone how you think she "should feel," or trying to make a decision for her. It is hard to break habits that we've had for many years. But, fortunately, we *can* change our behavior. With enough practice, skills such as acknowledging feelings and listening actively will come naturally. By polishing these skills we can become better communicators, and when friends or loved ones need support after a loss, we can be prepared to offer them help.

I ached with fear and anxiousness
and sought the counsel of my friends.
One quoted scripture and platitudes of God
But still the ache remained.
The other, with eyes and words said:
"I understand. I, too, have hurt."
I was soothed and calmed and healed.

◆

Judy Haralson[1]

Chapter 3

Step 3
Support Through
the Stages of Grief

After the verb to love, to help is the most beautiful
verb in the world.

◆ Countess Bertan Von Suttner

No two people grieve in exactly the same way. But research has shown that there are stages of grief which many people pass through following a loss. As discussed in Part I (Chapter 2), these are

◆ shock   ◆ anger

◆ panic   ◆ depression

◆ denial   ◆ returning

◆ release   ◆ hope

◆ guilt   ◆ acceptance

Not everyone experiences all the stages, and people do not always experience them in the same order. For example, some individuals never feel angry, while others may remain angry for what seems to be a long time.

Circumstances surrounding a loss may determine how the griever reacts. If a man's wife dies after a prolonged illness, for instance, he may not go through the shock stage. After all, he has had a long time to think about her death. On the other hand, the woman whose 40-year-old husband dies suddenly of a heart attack on the golf course may be in shock for weeks.

Being aware of these stages can be useful to you as a helper. As you observe the griever passing through these stages, you can assure him that his feelings—and actions—are normal. Grieving people often feel that they are "slipping," "cracking up" or "losing touch" when they experience panic, depression or guilt. But by helping the person recognize that these are actually steps of progress, he will be able to accept them and allow the healing to continue.

As you read the suggestions on the following pages for helping through the stages of grief, keep in mind that each person will experience grief in an individualized way. Don't be surprised if the person moves from denial to depression or from shock to anger.

In this chapter you will also learn about anniversary grief and unresolved grief, and how to help someone who may be experiencing the painful feelings associated with these forms of grieving.

Supporting Through the Stages of Grief

SHOCK

Be near the person and available to help. Do not take away tasks that she can do herself. Encourage her when this experience recurs from time to time. Remember, complete acceptance is a slow process.

> Griever: I don't know what's wrong with me. I just don't feel anything.
> Helper: Perhaps it's good not to feel so much right now.

> Griever: I'm just numb. I don't believe what has happened.
> Helper: It is really hard to accept this, isn't it?

PANIC

Assure the griever that his feelings of panic are normal, that he is not "cracking up." Answer only the necessary requests—keep everything simple. Encourage him in his movement toward the reality that grief work is hard but that he will survive. It may be necessary in time of panic to simply tell the person what to do with clear instructions. Talking things over may need to come at a later time.

> Griever: (Crying desperately)
> Helper: (Hold the person steadily and let the tears flow. Words are not necessary.)

> Griever: Help me! Help me! I can't stand to lose him.
> Helper: You feel desperate right now. (Hold the person gently.)

DENIAL

Stand by and help the person face the reality in small doses. Be observant of times when readiness appears on the surface. While denial should not continue for a lengthy period, we don't want to force the griever through this stage before she is ready. And remember, denial is often mistaken for bravery!

Griever: Oh, this kind of thing doesn't bother me.
Helper: You feel that everything is going to be all right.

Griever: Well, we'll make it through without difficulty.
Helper: It's hard to think about this right now.

RELEASE

Sit quietly and allow the person to release pent-up feelings. Show approval for this display. Do not try to stop this natural expression with "you mustn't cry, your loved one wouldn't want to see you this way."

Griever: I just can't stop crying.
Helper: That's okay, tears can sometimes be great healers.

Griever: I'm so tired, but I just can't seem to give up my morning run.
Helper: Exercise can be a healthy form of release, if you don't overdo it.

DEPRESSION

Help the griever accept the naturalness of this feeling. Remind her that "this, too, will pass." Express genuine concern but confidence in her ability to make it through this difficult time. Permission to experience depression in itself can make this stage of grieving more bearable.

Griever: I feel so lonely. I hate being alone.
Helper: Loneliness is a very painful part of losing.

Griever: I am so depressed. I shouldn't feel this way.
Helper: Feeling depressed is normal when you have lost something so important to you.

GUILT

Encourage the person to talk about her feelings of guilt. Let the griever know that these are natural feelings. Avoid any judgment such as "you shouldn't feel that way."

Griever: I wish I hadn't said that.
Helper: We all say things we don't mean.

Griever: If I had just studied harder, I might have passed that last test.
Helper: You must feel really disappointed about that.

ANGER

Help the person realize that these feelings are part of the grieving process. Create an atmosphere of acceptance in which the griever can comfortably "talk out" his anger and resentment. Avoid implying that he shouldn't be angry, and try not to defend the person or thing which is lost.

> Griever: I am so angry. I don't understand why this had to happen this way.
> Helper: Sometimes it's okay to be angry, really angry, about things we cannot control.

> Griever: I resent being left this way.
> Helper: It hurts to have somebody leave you.

RETURNING

Allow the person to continue to talk about the loss. Do not avoid mention of the loss as though it never happened. Demonstrate a personal interest in the returning process. Welcome the person "back."

> Griever: I am finally feeling better. I don't feel so angry anymore.
> Helper: It is good to feel that you are making it.

> Griever: It seems that sometimes I see a little light coming through.
> Helper: You're feeling good about that.

HOPE

Give warm affection, encouragement and support as the person begins experiencing life as meaningful again.

> Griever: I think I'll take that trip in the spring.
> Helper: Life is starting to come together for you again.

> Griever: It's been tough, but I think I'm going to make it.
> Helper: You have learned to survive.

ACCEPTANCE

People should not try to carry the burden of grief alone. They must be encouraged to grieve. Commend the person who has gotten to this stage of acceptance and discovered that he can live again and love again. Walk with him as he discovers the rays of sunshine becoming steadier. Affirm his grasping of reality and movement toward wholeness.

Griever: I wish it had never happened, but now that I have made it through, I have really learned a lot about life.

Helper: It must feel good to be able to go on.

Griever: If I could have changed things, I would have. But I've learned that I can't control everything.

Helper: You will never forget the experience, but you have certainly taken it and made it meaningful to yourself.

PHYSICAL SYMPTOMS

Although not one of the 10 stages, you will want to be aware of this. Accept the reality of the illness. The body does break down under excessive stress. Encourage medical care. Keep listening as the person works his way through the barriers. Counseling may be indicated.

Griever: I feel so sick. I just don't know what to do. I have a headache all the time.

Helper: Your body may be telling you that it's time to take care of yourself right now. You may want to see your doctor.

Griever: I am exhausted all the time.

Helper: You have been under a lot of stress. Perhaps you need to give your body some time off.

Anniversary Grief

For many, grieving is not only experienced at the actual time of the loss but also on a recurring basis.

Depression and other symptoms of grief may be experienced on

- ◆ birthdays
- ◆ holidays
- ◆ anniversaries of shared events
- ◆ anniversaries of the loss

The effective helper can

- assist in identifying the anniversary event
- review the stages of grief
- encourage the griever to experience the accompanying feelings

Example: **An effective helper**

Griever: I feel really lonely when I think of your father. We would have been married 15 years this June.

Helper: It seems that a lot of people experience those same feelings on anniversaries and other special dates—like the person's birthday.

Example: **An ineffective helper**

Griever: It's been almost a year since we moved.

Helper: Surely, you don't think about that anymore.

Rings and jewels are not gifts, but apologies for gifts. The only true gift is a portion of thyself.

◆ Ralph Waldo Emerson

Unresolved Grief

To be an effective helper, it is important to recognize grief that is left unresolved. This can be caused by

- denying the loss
- geographical separation
- maintaining a false image of strength
- ambivalence toward the loss
- not identifying the loss
- emotional inability to handle the loss

Example: **An effective helper**

Griever: I've been so busy with football practice, I haven't had time to think about Nancy breaking up with me.

Helper: Seems like it's still on your mind. Maybe it would be a good idea to take time out to think that through.

Example: **An ineffective helper**

Griever: I really don't want to go visit my father; I haven't thought about him much since he moved away after the divorce.

Helper: Oh, you'll get along all right. Don't worry about it.

You may recognize unresolved grief when

- the person still has difficulty talking about the loss
- new grief symptoms are obvious on the anniversary of the loss
- the person refuses to visit the grave or a place which reminds him of the loss
- the person is experiencing persistent guilt, depression or low self-esteem
- the person continues to look for or expect the return of the lost person
- the person overreacts to minor events, acting as though they were major losses
- the person puts other relationships in jeopardy

You may recognize grief that has been masked when

- the person continues with unidentified depression
- the person continues with extreme overwork
- there is an excessive amount of giddiness or flippancy
- the person remains withdrawn
- the person continually lacks energy
- the person continually denies that anything is wrong
- the person acts with bravado and insists, "That doesn't bother me."

How can the helper assist the griever in facing the reality of the loss?

- Listen carefully for clues; with the right opportunity, you might interject a reality statement.

- ◆ Be extremely sensitive to the person's "readiness" for help.
- ◆ Suggest professional help gently.
- ◆ Stand by.
- ◆ Remind the person that grieving is an acceptable behavior following a loss.
- ◆ Acknowledge that grieving can be frightening and painful.

A person has the ability to help another only when there is a constant willingness to feel one's pain and suffering knowing that this rises from the depth of the human condition which all of us share.

What are some additional ways of helping a person grieve over his losses? Think of methods which have been helpful to you. _____

_____

_____

_____

How can you help a person "get on with" the grieving? _____

_____

_____

_____

What can you do for the person who is denying/negating the loss? (Remember that denial is a defense mechanism that helps cushion the impact of the blow for a while. Do not take away the denial too quickly, but encourage professional help if it continues too long.)

_____

What can you do for the person who is geographically separated from a support system? _____

_____

What can you do for the person who thinks she *must* be strong and brave, to act "in control"? _____

_____

What can you do for the person who is unable to identify the loss? _____

_____

Melody

The melody that the loved one played upon the piano of your life will never be played quite that way again, but we must not close the keyboard and allow the instrument to gather dust.

◆   Joshua Loth Leibman,
Peace of Mind [1]

Chapter 4

Step 4
Encourage Healthy Coping Skills

Looking forward always means letting go.

◆

*A*s the person is experiencing the stages of grief, you may want to discuss outlets that have helped her to work through difficult times in the past. By using these coping techniques, or new ones, the person may be able to move more easily into the final stages: returning, hope and reality.

The griever may have a natural tendency to turn to a hobby, sport or favorite pastime to allow herself to work through the grief. But she may get "stuck" and need a few suggestions to help her move along. It is important that she choose what works for her, and that may be very different from what works for you. Some positive methods for coping may be suggested in this way:

◆ Sarah, it seems that you enjoy walking in the park.
That must bring you a lot of comfort.

◆ John, what do you enjoy doing that seems to bring you the most comfort—or maybe clears your mind for awhile?

◆ Tim, I've noticed that you have continued with your regular running schedule, and that makes sense. Exercise can bring a lot of relief.

A number of activities may relieve anxiety and bring comfort:

Crying • Working • Exercising • Reading • Talking
Joining a support group • Ritualizing • Reminiscing
Praying • Meditating • Using humor • Keeping a journal
or diary to record feelings and thoughts

List other activities that you think might be helpful or that you personally have found helpful in coping with grief.

_____

_____

_____

_____

_____

Life is filled with lessons on waiting —the hardest being the lesson on waiting on ourselves. We want to hurry out of the shadows, out of the valley, back to the sunshine and the mountain tops.

Be careful to discourage destructive ways of coping such as

- ◆ drinking alcoholic beverages
- ◆ using drugs without medical supervision
- ◆ sleeping too much or too little
- ◆ smoking
- ◆ overeating/undereating
- ◆ overworking

In what other negative ways do people sometimes try to cope with grief? _____

_____

_____

The following story tells about a teenage boy who used a healthy coping technique to replace a negative one—thanks to a helpful friend.

◆ John and Patti had been going together for four years when Patti suddenly decided she wanted to "play the field." John was shattered and proceeded to go out every night for two weeks and get drunk—"to forget," he said. John had been writing a humorous column in the school newspaper for two years. A close friend on the staff was concerned about John's destructive behavior and suggested that he write about what had happened in his column. The friend's idea worked: John turned out one of his best stories of the year—"It Hurts To Be Dumped Near the Dump!" (Patti had indeed delivered her bad news to John near the school dumpster.) By using his sense of humor, John gained a new perspective on the situation and was able to move out of his depression.

Models for Grieving

In helping someone cope with grief, it is sometimes useful to find out about his background. What kind of models did he have for grieving? How did relatives and others in his community deal with loss? By asking these kinds of questions, you may begin to understand the person's approach to mourning and be better equipped to offer him support. All of these factors may affect how a person handles loss:

- ◆ Family background
- ◆ Culture

- ◆ Religious training
- ◆ Faith and spiritual beliefs
- ◆ Health
- ◆ Support systems
- ◆ Knowledge and understanding

The beauty is made with music only when the pauses and rests are in the right places —thus enhancing the harmony.

Questions which might be appropriate in learning about the griever's background are:

- ◆ Tell me something about your family. How did they handle loss and how did they mourn?

- ◆ In your geographical area, what customs seem to influence grieving?

- ◆ From your church background or religious belief, how do you interpret what has happened?

- ◆ How do you see your health as a factor in handling this experience?

- ◆ Who are the people closest to you who are nurturing you?

- ◆ Are you familiar with the stages of grief and how your feelings fit into these stages?

- ◆ How has this loss affected your faith?

Use these questions one or two at a time. The entire list would be threatening. Remember that probing blocks communication.

Once you have gathered this information, you will be in a better position to discuss coping mechanisms. If the person's background or religion strictly forbids any form of socializing for a certain time period following a death, then you would not want to suggest that the person accept an invitation to a cocktail party to "get her mind off herself."

Coping mechanisms are more likely to be positive and bring the desired result when they are in keeping with the person's belief system, cultural background or religion. And, as emphasized earlier in this chapter, it is best to let the griever choose a method of coping for herself. As with so many of the aspects of helping discussed in this book, no one should be making decisions for a grieving person. But as they heal, many people who have experienced loss will welcome suggestions and support.

Chapter 5

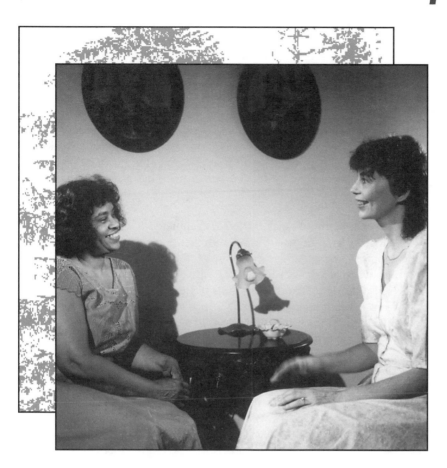

Step 5
Help With a
Plan of Action

Loving again
Trusting again
Starting anew
Developing new interests

◆

Sometimes, grieving people need to make important choices and decisions before they have completely healed. Making decisions can be difficult at any time, but it can be particularly hard for the person who has gone through a recent loss.

◆ Tanya, a young woman who had completed a doctoral program in English literature, had wanted to teach English at the college level for many years. When she completed her degree, she began applying for jobs at colleges and universities. After many "rejection" letters and six months of being unemployed, Tanya went into a grieving period. She realized that her dream for the future might never be fulfilled. And she faced the reality that she was going to have to seek some other kind of work.

◆ Harold, a 65-year-old man, was retiring. He and his wife had bought their dream condominium in Florida. As soon as he retired, they planned to move and leave their home of 35 years. But suddenly Harold's wife Linda died. Harold faced retirement in three months, and he had to decide whether to go on with the plan to move. It was a tough choice: To move to a city where he knew only a few people, or to remain in his home where he did at least have a support system.

If you are in a position to help someone explore future choices after a loss, it is helpful to follow a plan. Using the active listening skills discussed in Chapter 2, discuss the situation with the grieving person:

◆ Help the person identify the specific decision that needs immediate attention.

◆ Have the person brainstorm as many ways of handling the decision as possible.

◆ Assist the griever in evaluating the pros and cons of each alternative.

◆ Have the griever choose the alternative which *he* thinks is most workable.

◆ Encourage him to make a commitment to begin.

◆ Set a time for follow-up and evaluation of the plan.

As you are helping someone explore alternatives, try not to give advice. In giving advice, you are taking away the responsibility from the person you are helping. This reduces the learning process which will help him with future problems. By imposing your own solution, which may not be the choice of the griever, you also make yourself responsible if the plan fails.

Develop a Plan of Action

Some steps to take as you help the griever develop a plan of action:

1. Ask these questions:

    What is the decision to be made?

    What are the alternatives?

    What are the consequences of each alternative?

2. Hypothesize which alternative is most likely to work out satisfactorily.

3. Set a time to discuss and evaluate.

    If the griever can't think of alternatives, you may comment:

    Have you considered _____ ?

    Wonder what would happen if you tried _____ .

    What do you think would happen if _____ ?

    Have you thought of the possibility of _____ ?

When offering suggestions, be sure to

    ◆ leave room for choices

- leave the responsibility of making the final decision with the griever

- leave the griever with feelings of satisfaction about her own choice

Summarizing and Clarifying

When you spend time with the griever, listen and respond as he discusses his plan of action—it may help for you to clarify and summarize what he is saying. Condense the key themes, topics, conflicts or decisions to be made. Make your summaries tentative and invite corrections.

. . . wounds and pain become openings or occasions for a new vision.

Henri Nouwen,
The Wounded Healer [1]

Summarizing and clarifying

- enables you to keep all the information straight

- allows the griever the chance to organize his thinking

- gives you an opportunity to correct your interpretations

- lets the griever know you have been listening

To summarize the issue at hand, briefly restate what you believe the person is saying. Try one of these methods:

- It seems as if the situation is _____ .

- After all this, you are trying to decide _____ .

- It sounds as though you are saying _____ .

- This is what I think I am hearing _____ .

To clarify the situation, and possibly provide the griever with additional insight, one of these questions may help:

- Can you tell me more about that?

- Would you like to talk about that some more?

◆ I'd be interested to know what you have worked out about that.

◆ How do you feel about that?

◆ Can you be more specific about that?

◆ Could you help me understand that more clearly?

For practice, look back over the steps involved in "Develop a Plan of Action." Keeping in mind that summarizing and clarifying may help, think about how you would work with Tanya on her career decision (page 122).

What does Tanya need to decide? _____

_____

What might you discuss with her before ever getting to the "Develop a Plan of Action" stage? _____

_____

_____

In taking the journey towards healing, I am taking risky steps through unmarked territory.

Would it help to know about Tanya's other interests besides teaching?

_____

If Tanya cannot come up with alternatives, what would be a few options that you might suggest to her? _____

_____

_____

_____

Now, let's consider Harold's decision (page 122).

What are some alternatives for Harold? _____

_____

_____

_____

_____

What are possible consequences of some of these alternatives?

_____

_____

_____

_____

Failure to make necessary decisions and to act after a major loss can create more problems for the person who is grieving.

Although every loss does not require immediate action, when decisions must be made it is helpful to have someone to think them through with.

In life you cannot establish the curriculum, you can only choose which course to take.

◆ E. Kennedy

Chapter 6

Step 6
Guide Toward Finding Meaning

What makes a meaningful life? The answers are within a person. That meaning makes me what I am. Facing death means facing the ultimate question of the meaning of life.

◆

*T*he griever will be searching diligently for some reasonable explanation of the loss. Along with the anger, guilt, depression and loneliness will undoubtedly come the question, *why*. We all need to believe that suffering has some ultimate meaning or that it offers us a learning experience.

A loss can take away faith in God or strengthen it. It can rob us of our childhood innocence—our thinking that good behavior brings rewards. It can cloud our belief in the goodness of the world.

How then can we answer these questions:

- ◆ Can loss be educational?
- ◆ Can it make us better?
- ◆ Can it cure our faults?
- ◆ Is "Why did this happen to me?" the right question?

There may be *no answer*, but by encouraging the griever to ask questions, we can help him clarify how he feels and move toward finding meaning. Each of us must search for our own meaning to life's experiences. As a helper, you can stand by while this reality begins to emerge, watching lovingly as the person slowly makes his way out of the sorrow and into the light of hope, acceptance and reality. But it is important not to force the griever to begin this process. Readiness is essential at this stage. Be sure to allow him time to vent emotions before he begins to think about the meaning in his loss.

Working through the pain of loss toward rebirth is dependent on our internal motivation to grow. If we are robbed of the journey by those who want to rush us or do it for us, we miss the long-term healing that is rightfully ours.

In order to find meaning in a loss, the griever will have to choose to give the experience purpose and to listen for the lessons. As he moves into the stages of hope, acceptance and reality, he can ask himself some questions:

◆ Although I cannot change what happened, now that it has happened, what am I going to do with it?

◆ I don't like what has happened, but what am I going to do with the rest of my life?

◆ As this door has closed, where is the next one opening?

When the time is right, you can begin to help the griever look for the purpose which can enrich his life. As Harold Kushner tells us in his book, *When Bad Things Happen to Good People*, "When I think of what I have gained, yesterday seems less painful and I am not afraid of tomorrow."

Encourage the griever as he turns the loss into a meaningful experience. One of the following questions or statements may help:

◆ As you look at this experience, is it possible that you have found new meaning in relationships that you were not aware of before?

◆ Have you considered your growth during this time, the changes in you which this loss seems to have brought?

◆ Do you think now that you have learned so much that you would be willing to go back to the way you used to be?

◆ Would you be comfortable to just stay where you are, or do you feel that you are now ready to take another step forward?

◆ How has the experience changed your life?

◆ How has it influenced your life purpose and belief system?

◆ What positive action have you taken or might you take as a result of this lesson?

- ◆ You seem to have learned that there are a lot of things over which we have no control.

- ◆ You have gained a lot of self-confidence in your ability to handle a crisis.

There is a beginning and an ending for everything that is alive. In between is living.

Bryan Mellonie and Robert Ingpen, *Lifetimes, The Beautiful Way To Explain Death To Children* [1]

- ◆ You seem to feel that with all the loss, you are gaining a kind of independence that you never knew you could enjoy.

- ◆ I like to hear you laugh; it seems that you are more able to express your feelings since your recent experience.

It is important for us to avoid making statements that would block the griever's struggle to find meaning in the loss.

Comments such as these may do more harm than good:

- ■ As you look at this, you have no doubt learned never to do it again.

- ■ Life's lessons are hard, and you have certainly made this one into a hard one.

- ■ When you make mistakes, you always have to pay.

- ■ If you had kept in touch, you wouldn't feel so bad.

- ■ You'll learn from this one to be kind from now on.

- ■ I do hope you've learned your lesson.

- ■ Everything will be all right.

What are some other observations you might make, or questions you might ask, that could help the griever in her search for meaning? _____

_____

As we identify our losses, weave through the pain, reflect upon their meaning and move into the healing, the fragments of our lives begin to come together and life begins to make sense again.

◆

Possible Meanings

The following list of possible meanings may aid you in guiding the griever toward discovery:

You have learned . . .

- that you can love.
- that loving hurts.
- that you can survive.
- that healing occurs.
- that you have grown.
- that you can forgive.
- that change is a necessary part of life.
- that you wouldn't miss the person if he/she hadn't been so important to you.
- that the person taught you a lot.
- that you are grateful for the many things the person gave you.
- that you like sharing your space.
- that you can be a receiver.
- that you cannot control everything.
- that you can open your space.
- that you can care.
- that you can become involved.
- that you need a significant other.
- that you can re-evaluate yourself.
- that you can check out your behavior patterns.
- to look at relationships more seriously.

Life can never again be the way it was. If you have learned and grown, you can never be the same again.

Joyce Rupp,
Praying our Goodbyes [2]

131

Enjoying solitude

Creating
Appreciating
Meditating
Growing
Moving on

◆ to look at attitudes.

◆ to look at weakness as a possible strength.

◆ to be more in touch with your feelings.

◆ to express your feelings more clearly.

◆ to appreciate life more.

◆ to appreciate this disruption in your life as motivation to grow.

◆ that a new chapter in your life is being written.

◆ that you will have to change.

◆ to experiment with new life-styles.

◆ that you can start again.

◆ new ways of filling your days.

◆ to enjoy "aloneness."

◆ to tap resources of courage.

◆ that you are a richer person.

◆ that you are wiser.

◆ that you have discovered a new level of courage.

◆ that you are more open.

◆ that love is for you.

◆ that you can make new contacts on your own.

◆ that you can gain self-confidence.

◆ that you are basically a social being.

◆ that you can expand your world.

◆ that you can ask for support.

◆ that you have the courage to allow yourself to feel.

◆ that you can still enjoy a sunset.

- ◆ that you are different.
- ◆ that you have evolved.
- ◆ that you are stronger, more independent, happier.
- ◆ that you are learning to like the independence.
- ◆ that you have choices.
- ◆ that you can make choices.
- ◆ that the person will always be an essential part of your life.
- ◆ the value and importance of the present.

As the griever continues in the direction of hope and acceptance, he may look back in great surprise at the lessons he has learned.

What kinds of lessons have you learned through loss? _____

_____

_____

_____

Do you recall how you reached your conclusions? Did you read something that was inspirational, or did someone say something that led you to your belief? _____

_____

_____

_____

What insights have others you know gained through the experience of loss? _____

_____

_____

_____

_____

_____

_____

Conclusion

Helping someone "survive" after a loss by sharing his pain is often difficult. But it can be equally rewarding. We may gain insights throughout the helping process that ultimately affect our own lives. We will surely enrich our relationship with the person we have helped. It is perhaps that feeling of "connectedness" with another human being that will be most meaningful—and satisfying—to us. Goethe,  the German philosopher, beautifully expressed the importance of this kind of intimate interaction:

The world is so empty

If one thinks only

Of mountains, rivers and cities;

But to know someone

Here and there

Who thinks and feels with us,

And who, though distant,

Is close to us in spirit,

This makes the earth for us

An inhabited garden.

◆　　Goethe

Chapter Notes

Part I: When You Have Lost

CHAPTER 1. WHAT HAVE YOU LOST?

1. Joyce Rupp, *Praying Our Goodbyes* (Notre Dame, IN: Maria Press, 1988).

2. Melba Colgrove, et al., *How to Survive the Loss of a Love* (New York: Leo Press, 1976).

CHAPTER 2. HOW DO YOU REACT?

1. Anne Morrow-Lindbergh, *Hour of Gold, Hour of Lead* (New York: Harcourt, Brace & Jovanovich, 1973).

2. Scott Peck, *The Road Less Traveled* (New York: Simon and Schuster, Inc., 1978).

3. Joyce Rupp, *Praying Our Goodbyes* (Notre Dame, IN: Maria Press, 1988).

4. Ibid.

5. Scott Peck, *The Road Less Traveled* (New York: Simon and Schuster, Inc., 1978).

CHAPTER 3. HOW DO YOU COPE?

1. Elisabeth Kubler-Ross, *Death, The Final Stage of Growth* (Englewood Cliffs, NJ: Prentice-Hall, Inc., 1975).

2. Taken from *Praying Our Goodbyes* by Joyce Rupp, osm. Copyright 1988 by Maria Press, Notre Dame, IN 46556. All rights reserved. Used with permission of the publisher.

Part II: When You Want To Help

CHAPTER 1. STEP 1 - BE AVAILABLE

1. Leo Buscaglia, *The Fall of Freddie the Leaf* (Therofare, NJ: Charles B. Slack, Inc., 1982).

CHAPTER 2. STEP 2 - COMMUNICATE CARING AND CONCERN

1. Judy Haralson, Austin, Texas. Poem used with written permission of the author.

CHAPTER 3. STEP 3 - SUPPORT THROUGH THE STAGES OF GRIEF

1. Joshua Loth Leibman, *Peace of Mind* (New York: Simon and Schuster, Inc.,1946).

CHAPTER 5. STEP 5 - HELP WITH A PLAN OF ACTION

1. Henri Nouwen, *The Wounded Healer* (Garden City, NJ: Image Book, a division of Doubleday & Co., Inc., 1979).

CHAPTER 6. STEP 6 - GUIDE TOWARD FINDING MEANING

1. Bryan Mellonie and Robert Ingpen, *Lifetimes, The Beautiful Way To Explain Death To Children* (New York: Bantam Books, 1983).

2. Joyce Rupp, *Praying Our Goodbyes* (Notre Dame, IN: Maria Press, 1988).

For clarification, all unreferenced quotes throughout this book are written by Mary Joe Hannaford.

References

Babbitt, Natalie. *Tuck Everlasting*. Toronto, Canada: Collins Publishers, 1975.

Behensee, Barbara, and Jane Pequette. *Perspectives on Loss*. Evergreen, CO.

Bolton, Iris. *My Son, My Son*. Atlanta, GA: Bolton Press, 1983.

Buscaglia, Leo. *The Fall of Freddie the Leaf*. Therofare, NJ: Charles B. Slack, Inc., 1982.

Claypool, John. *Tracks of a Fellow Struggler*. Waco, TX: Word Books Publisher, 1974.

Clifton, Lucille. *Everett Anderson's Goodbye*. New York, NY: Henry Holt & Co., Inc., 1983.

Colgrove, et al. *How to Survive the Loss of a Love*. New York, NY: Leo Press, 1976.

Dye, Harold E. *Through God's Eyes*. Nashville, TN: Broadman Press, 1947.

Frassler, Joan. *My Grandpa Died Today*. New York, NY: Human Sciences Press, 1971.

Furman, Erna. *A Child's Parent Dies*. New Haven, CT: Yale University Press, 1974.

Ginott, Haim G. *Between Parent and Child*. New York, NY: Avon Books, 1965.

Gordon, Sol. *When Living Hurts*. New York, NY: Dell Publishing, 1983.

Grollman, Earl A. *Explaining Death to Children*. Boston, MA: Beacon Press, 1969.

Hannaford, Mary Joe. *The Joy of Sorrow*. Atlanta, GA: Pettit Publications, 1983.

Iaves, Isabella. *Love Must Not Be Wasted*. New York, NY: Crowell, 1974.

Kubler-Ross, Elisabeth. *Death, The Final Stage of Growth*. Englewood Cliffs, NJ: Prentice-Hall, Inc., 1975.

Kubler-Ross, Elisabeth. *On Death and Dying*. New York, NY: MacMillan Publishing Co., 1974.

Kushner, Harold S. *When Bad Things Happen to Good People*. New York, NY: Avon Books, 1981.

Leibman, Joshua Loth. *Peace of Mind*. New York, NY: Simon and Schuster, Inc., 1946.

Lewis, C.S. *The Problem of Pain*. New York, NY: MacMillan Publishing, 1962.

Mellonie, Bryan, and Robert Ingpen. *Lifetimes, The Beautiful Way To Explain Death To Children*. New York, NY : Bantam Books, 1983.

Middelton-Moz, Jane, and Lorie Dwinell. *After the Tears*. Deerfield Beach, FL: Health Communications, Inc., 1986.

Moody, Raymond A., Jr. *Life After Life*. St. Simons, GA: Mockingbird Books, 1975.

Morrow-Lindbergh, Anne. *Hour of Gold, Hour of Lead*. New York, NY: Harcourt, Brace & Jovanovich, 1973.

Nouwen, Henri. *The Wounded Healer*. Garden City, NJ: Image Books, a division of Doubleday & Co., Inc., 1979.

Ozment, Robert V. *When Sorrow Comes*. Waco, TX: Word Books Publisher, 1973.

Paulus, Trinn. *Hope for the Flowers*. New York, NY: Paulist Press, 1972.

Peck, Scott. *The Road Less Traveled*. New York, NY: Simon and Schuster, Inc., 1978.

Pincus, Lily. *Death and the Family*. New York, NY: Vintage Books, 1974.

Raines, Robert A. *Lord, Could You Make It a Little Better*. Waco, TX: Word Books Publisher, 1972.

Reid, Clyde. *Celebrate the Temporary*. New York, NY: Harper and Row, 1972.

Rupp, Joyce. *Praying Our Goodbyes*. Notre Dame, IN: Maria Press, 1988.

Smith, Doris Buchanan. *A Taste of Blackberries*. New York, NY: Crowell, 1973.

Sullender, R. Scott. *Grief and Growth*. New York, NY: Paulist Press, 1985.

Temes, Roberta. *Living With an Empty Chair*. New York, NY: Irvington Pub., 1977.

Viorst, Judith. *Necessary Losses*. New York, NY: Fawcett Gold Medal, 1986.

Weatherhead, Leslie D. *The Will of God*. New York, NY: Abingdon Press, 1944.

Westberg, Granger, E. *Good Grief*. Philadelphia, PA: Fortress Press, 1971.

NOTES

NOTES

NOTES

NOTES

NOTES

NOTES